The Inhuman

The Inhuman

Reflections on Time

Jean-François Lyotard

Translated by Geoffrey Bennington and Rachel Bowlby

Stanford University Press
Stanford, California
1991

Stanford University Press
Stanford, California
© 1988 Editions Galilée as *L'Inhuman: Causeries sur le temps*
English translation © 1991 Polity Press
Originating publisher of English edition: Polity
   Press in association with Basil Blackwell Publishers,
   Oxford
First published in the U.S.A. by Stanford
   University Press
Printed in Great Britain
Cloth ISBN 0-8047-2006-1
Paper ISBN 0-8047-2008-8
LC 91-66838

This book is printed on acid-free paper

Contents

Preface and Acknowledgements

Full bibliographical details of each chapter are given below.

1 Text based on the recording of a session of the seminar held at the Graduiertenkolleg of the University of Siegen, Germany, at the invitation of its director, Hans Ulrich Gumbrecht. This translation is reprinted from *Discourse* II: 1 (1987). Translated by Bruce Boone and Lee Hildreth.

2 Modified text of a paper given at the University of Wisconsin, Milwaukee and Madison, in April 1986. Earlier English version published in *Substance*, Autumn 1987; the French version from which this translation was made was published in the *Cahiers de philosophie*, 5 (1988).

3 Extract from the seminar on 'Matter and the immaterials' held in April 1985 in the Seminar Space of the Georges Pompidou Centre, Paris, on the initiative of its director, Christian Descamps. The other participants in the seminar were Francis Bailly, Fernando Gil, Vittorio Gregotti, Dominique Lecourt, Fernando Montes, Jean Petitot, Paolo Portoghesi and Gianni Vattimo. This translation reprinted from 'Matter and Time' in *Philosophy and the Visual Arts*, Academy Editions, London, 1990.

4 Paper given to the conference on 'New technologies and the mutation of knowledge, organized in October 1986

for the Collège International de Philosophie and IRCAM by Bernard Stiegler.

5 Rewritten text based on a paper given in July 1987 to the Carl Friedrich von Siemens Stiftung in Munich, on the invitation of its administrative director, Heinrich Meier, in the context of a course entitled 'Zur Diagnose der Moderne'. Published in French in *Critique*, 493–4 (June–July 1988). This translation reprinted from *OLR* 11 (1989).

6 Text taken from the catalogue of the exhibition 'Time: looking at the fourth dimension', organized by Michel Baudson, directeur adjoint of the Society of Exhibitions at the Palais des Beaux-Arts in Brussels. Reprinted in *Po&sie*, 34 (1985). This translation by David Macey is reprinted from 'Newman: The Instant', in Andrew Benjamin (ed.), *The Lyotard Reader* (Oxford: Blackwell, 1989), by kind permission of the publisher.

7 Lecture given at the Kunsthochshule in Berlin in January 1983, preceded by the German translation read by Heike Rutke (co-translator with Clemens Carl Härle), which was published in *Merkur* 38:2 March 1984. French text translated here was published in *Po&sie*, 34 (1985). This translation was first published in *Art Forum*, 22, part 8 (April 1984), in a translation by Lisa Liebmann, which is reproduced with kind permission. Alterations were made to the French text by Jean-François Lyotard when he gave the paper in Cambridge in March 1984, and these have been translated by Geoff Bennington and Marian Hobson and incorporated into the translation.

8 Lecture given to the first 'Art and communication' conference, organized by Robert Allezaud at the Sorbonne in October 1985, and published under his editorship in *Art et communication* (Paris: éditions Osiris, 1986).

9 Modified text of an article first published in an English translation by Lisa Liebmann at the request of Ingrid Sischy, in *Artforum*, 20:8 (1988).

10 From the catalogue of the exhibition 'Photographs of the Salpêtrière', organized by Franco Cagnetta in the spring of 1980 in Venice. Published in *Furor*, 4 (October 1981).

11 Text rewritten on the basis of a paper given to the conference 'The states of theory', held at the University of California, Irvine, in April 1987, under the aegis of the Focused Research Program in Contemporary Critical Theory, under its director Murray Krieger.

12 Paper given to the conference 'Museum/Memorial', organized by Jean-Louis Déotte under the aegis of the Bibliothèque Publique d'Information and the Collège International de Philosophie, at the Georges Pompidou Centre, Paris, in October 1986.

13 Paper presented to the conference 'Music and repetition', organized by Marie-Louise Mallet under the aegis of the Collège International de Philosophie in Lyon, January 1987.

14 Paper presented to the conference 'On musical writing', organized by Christine Buci-Glucksmann and Michaël Levinas under the aegis of the Collège International de Philosophie and L'Itineraire at the Sorbonne, June 1986. Published in *InHarmoniques*, 1 (1987).

15 Published in the *Revue des sciences humaines*, 1 (1988) in a special issue on 'Writing the Landscape', edited by Jean-Marc Besse. This translation by David Macey reprinted from 'Scapeland' in Andrew Benjamin (ed.), *The Lyotard Reader* (Oxford: Blackwell, 1989), by kind permission.

16 Paper given to the conference 'Le non sens commun', organized by Paolo Fabbri, Maurizio Ferraris, Jean-François Lyotard and Pino Paioni, under the aegis of the Centro Internazionale di Semiotica e di Linguistica and the Collège International de Philosophie, Urbino, July 1987. Published in *Po&sie*, 44 (1988).

Introduction: About the Human

Humanism administers lessons to 'us' (?). In a million ways, often mutually incompatible. Well founded (Apel) and non-founded (Rorty), counterfactual (Habermas, Rawls) and pragmatic (Searle), psychological (Davidson) and ethico-political (the French neo-humanists). But always as if at least man were a certain value, which has no need to be interrogated. Which even has the authority to suspend, forbid interrogation, suspicion, the thinking which gnaws away at everything.

What *value* is, what *sure* is, what *man* is, these questions are taken to be dangerous and shut away again pretty fast. It is said that they open the way to 'anything goes', 'anything is possible', 'all is worthless'. Look, they add, what happens to the ones who go beyond this limit: Nietzsche taken hostage by fascist mythology, Heidegger a Nazi, and so on . . . .

Even what may be worrying in Kant from this point of view, what is not anthropological but properly transcendental, and what, in the critical tension, goes so far as to break up the more or less presupposed unity of a (human) subject, as is the case – to me exemplary – of the analysis of the sublime or the historico-political writings, even that gets expurgated. On the pretext of a return to Kant, all they do is to shelter the humanist prejudice under his authority.

A similar movement of restoration is also attacking the writing and reading of texts, and the visual arts and architecture. In the name of norm-bound public reception, Jauss refuses the text of Adorno: the writing of the *Aesthetic*

1

Theory, twisted, uncertain, almost haggard, is judged unreadable. Be communicable, that is the prescription. Avant-garde is old hat, talk about humans in a human way, address yourself to human beings, if they enjoy receiving you then they will receive you.

It is not that humanism is simply a marketing operation. Those who tell 'us' (?) off are not all culture-industry hacks. They also call themselves philosophers. But what *philosophy* is must not be interrogated either, at the risk of falling into who knows what. I am not dreaming: the aim of the avant-gardes (dreadful name, I know) is something that they declared on numerous occasions. In 1913, Apollinaire wrote ingenuously: 'More than anything, artists are men who want to become inhuman.' And in 1969, Adorno again, more prudently: 'Art remains loyal to humankind uniquely through its inhumanity in regard to it.'

The 'talks' collected here – they are all commissioned lectures, mostly destined for a non-professional audience, and the rest for confiding – have neither the function nor the value of a manifesto or treatise. The suspicion they betray (in both senses of this word) is simple, although double: what if human beings, in humanism's sense, were in the process of, constrained into, becoming inhuman (that's the first part)? And (the second part), what if what is 'proper' to humankind were to be inhabited by the inhuman?

Which would make two sorts of inhuman. It is indispensable to keep them dissociated. The inhumanity of the system which is currently being consolidated under the name of development (among others) must not be confused with the infinitely secret one of which the soul is hostage. To believe, as happened to me, that the first can take over from the second, give it expression, is a mistake. The system rather has the consequence of causing the forgetting of what escapes it. But the anguish is that of a mind haunted by a familiar and unknown guest which is agitating it, sending it delirious but also making it think – if one claims to exclude it, if one doesn't give it an outlet, one aggravates it. Discontent grows with this civilization, foreclosure along with information.

Many of these lectures bear on the question of time. The reason is that it is decisive for the separation we are talking

about. Development imposes the saving of time. To go fast is
to forget fast, to retain only the information that is useful
afterwards, as in 'rapid reading'. But writing and reading
which advance backwards in the direction of the unknown
thing 'within' are slow. One loses one's time seeking time lost.
Anamnesis is the other pole – not even that, there is no
common axis – the *other* of acceleration and abbreviation.

Let's illustrate this with a word about an 'example' which
is in fact exemplary, and accessible to the humanists:
education. If humans are born human, as cats are born cats
(within a few hours), it would not be ... I don't even say
desirable, which is another question, but simply possible, to
educate them. That children have to be educated is a
circumstance which only proceeds from the fact that they are
not completely led by nature, not programmed. The institutions which constitute culture supplement this native lack.

What shall we call human in humans, the initial misery of
their childhood, or their capacity to acquire a 'second' nature
which, thanks to language, makes them fit to share in
communal life, adult consciousness and reason? That the
second depends on and presupposes the first is agreed by
everyone. The question is only that of knowing whether this
dialectic, whatever name we grace it with, leaves no remainder.

If this were the case, it would be inexplicable for the adult
himself or herself not only that s/he has to struggle constantly
to assure his or her conformity to institutions and even to
arrange them with a view to a better living-together, but that
the power of criticizing them, the pain of supporting them
and the temptation to escape them persist in some of his or
her activities. I do not mean only symptoms and particular
deviancies, but what, in our civilization at least, passes as
institutional: literature, the arts, philosophy. There too, it is a
matter of traces of an indetermination, a childhood, persist-
ing up to the age of adulthood.

It is a consequence of these banal observations that one can
take pride in the title of humanity for exactly opposite
reasons. Shorn of speech, incapable of standing upright,
hesitating over the objects of its interest, not able to calculate
its advantages, not sensitive to common reason, the child is

3

eminently the human because its distress heralds and promises things possible. Its initial delay in humanity, which makes it the hostage of the adult community, is also what manifests to this community the lack of humanity it is suffering from, and which calls on it to become more human.

But endowed with the means of knowing and making known, of doing and getting done, having interiorized the interests and values of civilization, the adult can pretend to full humanity in his or her turn, and to the effective realization of mind as consciousness, knowledge and will. That it always remains for the adult to free himself or herself from the obscure savageness of childhood by bringing about its promise – that is precisely the condition of humankind.

So between the two versions of humanism, there would only be a difference of emphasis. A well-ordered dialectic or hermeneutics hasten to come along and harmonize them. In short, our contemporaries find it adequate to remind us that what is proper to humankind is its absence of defining property, its nothingness, or its transcendence, to display the sign 'no vacancy'.

I do not like this haste. What it hurries, and crushes, is what after the fact I find I have always tried, under diverse headings – work, figural, heterogeneity, dissensus, event, thing – to reserve: the unharmonizable. (And I am not the only one, which is why I write 'us'.) That a senseless difference be *destined* to making sense, as opposition in a system, to talk structuralist, is one thing; another is that it is *promised* to the becoming-system. As if reason had no doubt that its vocation is to draw on the indeterminate to give it form, and that it cannot fail to succeed in this. Yet it is only at the price of this doubt that reason reasons.

This, we might say, is a basic motive for keeping at a distance any form of reconciliatory speculation. The appreciation of the contemporary situation provides another nourishment for this reserve. We should first remember that if the name of human can and must oscillate between native indetermination and instituted or self-instituting reason, it is the same for the name of inhuman. All education is inhuman because it does not happen without constraint and terror; I mean the least controlled, the least pedagogical

4

terror, the one Freud calls castration and which makes him say, in relation to the 'good way' of bringing up children, that in any case it will be bad (close in this to Kantian melancholy). And conversely, everything in the instituted which, in the event, can cut deep with distress and indetermination is so threatening that the reasonable mind cannot fail to fear in it, and rightly, an inhuman power of deregulation.

But the stress thus placed on the conflict of inhumanities is legitimated, nowadays more than previously, by the fact of a transformation of the nature of the system which I believe is a profound one.

The Trans-formation ...

We have to try to understand this transformation, without pathos but also without negligence. We have to regard as an inconsistency thinking which takes no account of it and 'sets up' descriptions, even if counterfactual, which is to say ideal or utopian, and especially the first, as if there were nothing more preventing their realization or truth nowadays than two centuries ago. The term *postmodern* has been used, badly rather than well if I judge by the results, to designate something of this transformation.

It will be seen in the pages which follow how one can try to describe it following the general, positivist hypothesis of a process of complexification, negative entropy or, put more simply, development. This hypothesis is not only suggested by the convergence of tendencies animating all the sub-groups of contemporary activity, it is the very argument of the discourse maintained about their researches by the scientists, the technologists and their accredited philosophers to legitimate, scientifically and technologically, the possibility of their development. Inevitably, it is a discourse of general physics, with its dynamics, its economics, its cybernetics. Any discourse of general physics is a metaphysical discourse, as we have known since Aristotle and Leibniz.

This discourse is just as much the one which the political or socioeconomic decision-maker uses to legitimate his or her options: competitiveness, better distribution of costs, democracy in society, enterprise, school and family. Even the rights of man, which however came from a quite different horizon, can be appealed to in reinforcement of the authority of the

5

system, although it, according to the very way it is set up, can only make of them an episodic case.

I am not making this hypothesis about development my own, because it is a way, *the* way, for metaphysics, henceforth ruled out for thinking, to re-establish its rights over it. To re-establish them not *within* thinking (if I make an exception of the thinking which still calls itself philosophical, which is to say metaphysical), but *from the outside* of thinking. Metaphysics being impossible as such, it makes itself reality and thus acquires the rights *de facto*. This situation defines quite usefully what we used to call *ideology*, in that ideology is not remarkable so much as a system of ideas but rather as a power of realization. 'Development' is the ideology of the present time, it realizes the essential of metaphysics, which was a thinking pertaining to forces much more than to the subject.

Pursuing the argument just a little, as is done here, one concludes that the system by which native indetermination is constrained, 'forced', even if in the trappings of permissiveness, does not proceed from the reason of mankind, say of the Enlightenment. It results from a process of development, where it is not mankind which is the issue, but differentiation. This obeys a simple principle: between two elements, whatever they are, whose relation is given at the start, it is always possible to introduce a third term which will assure a better regulation. *Better* means more reliable, but also of greater capacity. The initial relation mediated in this way appears as a particular case in a series of possible regulations. Mediation does not only imply the alienation of elements as to their relation, it permits the modulation of that relation. And the 'richer' – i.e. itself mediated – the mediating term, the more numerous the possible modifications, the suppler the regulation, the more floating the rate of exchange between the elements, the more permissive the mode of relation.

The description is abstract. It could be illustrated easily from elements as apparently diverse as economic or social partners, the cells of an organ or organism, the constituents of the molecule or nucleus, monetary tender, opposing military powers. The new technologies and the media are aspects of the same differentiation.

6

The striking thing about this metaphysics of development is that it needs no finality. Development is not attached to an Idea, like that of the emancipation of reason and of human freedoms. It is reproduced by accelerating and extending itself according to its internal dynamic alone. It assimilates risks, memorizes their informational value and uses this as a new mediation necessary to its functioning. It has no necessity itself other than a cosmological chance.

It has thus no end, but it does have a limit, the expectation of the life of the sun. The anticipated explosion of this star is the only challenge objectively posed to development. The natural selection of systems is thus no longer of a biological, but of a cosmic order. It is to take up this challenge that all research, whatever its sector of application, is being set up already in the so-called developed countries. The interest of humans is subordinate in this to that of the survival of complexity.

And finally, since development is the very thing which takes away the hope of an alternative to the system from both analysis and practice, since the politics which 'we' have inherited from revolutionary modes of thought and actions now turns out to be redundant (whether we find this a cause for joy or a matter to be deplored), the question I am raising here is simply this: what else remains as 'politics' except resistance to this inhuman? And what else is left to resist with but the debt which each soul has contracted with the miserable and admirable indetermination from which it was born and does not cease to be born? – which is to say, with the other inhuman?

This debt to childhood is one which we never pay off. But it is enough not to forget it in order to resist it and perhaps, not to be unjust. It is the task of writing, thinking, literature, arts, to venture to bear witness to it.

7

1

Can Thought go on
without a Body?

HE

You philosophers ask questions without answers, questions
that have to remain unanswered to deserve being called
philosophical. According to you answered questions are only
technical matters. That's what they were to begin with. They
were mistaken for philosophical questions. You turn to other
questions that seem completely impossible to answer: which
by definition resist every attempt at conquest by the understanding. Or what amounts to the same thing: you declare if
the first questions were answered, that's because they were
badly formulated. And you grant yourselves the privilege of
continuing to regard as unresolved, that is as well formulated,
questions that technical science believes it answered but in
truth only inadequately dealt with. For you solutions are just
illusions, failures to maintain the integrity due to being – or
some such thing. Long live patience. You'll hold out forever
with your incredulity. But don't be surprised if all the same,
through your irresolution, you end up wearing out your reader.

But that's not the question. While we talk, the sun is getting
older. It will explode in 4.5 billion years. It's just a little
beyond the halfway point of its expected lifetime. It's like a
man in his early forties with a life expectancy of eighty. With
the sun's death your insoluble questions will be done with
too. It's possible they'll stay unanswered right up to the end,
flawlessly formulated, though now both grounds for raising

8

such questions as well as the place to do this will no longer exist. You explain: it's impossible to think an end, pure and simple, of anything at all, since the end's a limit and to think it you have to be on both sides of that limit. So what's finished or finite has to be perpetuated in our thought if it's to be thought of as finished. Now this is true of limits belonging to thought. But after the sun's death there won't be a thought to know that its death took place.

That, in my view, is the sole serious question to face humanity today. In comparison everything else seems insignificant. Wars, conflicts, political tension, shifts in opinion, philosophical debates, even passions – everything's dead already if this infinite reserve from which you now draw energy to defer answers, if in short thought as quest, dies out with the sun. Maybe death isn't the word. But the inevitable explosion to come, the one that's always forgotten in your intellectual ploys, can be seen in a certain way as coming before the fact to render these ploys posthumous – make them futile. I'm talking about what's X'd out of your writings – matter. Matter taken as an arrangement of energy created, destroyed and recreated over and over again, endlessly. On the corpuscular and/or cosmic scale I mean. I am not talking about the familiar, reassuring terrestrial world or the reassuring transcendent immanence of thought to its objects, analogous to the way the eye transcends what's visible or *habitus* its *situs*. In 4.5 billion years there will arrive the demise of your phenomenology and your utopian politics, and there'll be no one there to toll the death knell or hear it. It will be too late to understand that your passionate, endless questioning always depended on a 'life of the mind' that will have been nothing else than a covert form of earthly life. A form of life that was spiritual because human, human because earthly – coming from the earth of the most living of living things. Thought borrows a horizon and orientation, the limitless limit and the end without end it assumes, from the corporeal, sensory, emotional and cognitive experience of a quite sophisticated but definitely earthly existence – to which it's indebted as well.

With the disappearance of earth, thought will have stopped – leaving that disappearance absolutely unthought of. It's the

9

horizon itself that will be abolished and, with its disappearance, your transcendence in immanence as well. If, as a limit, death really is what escapes and is deferred and as a result what thought has to deal with, right from the beginning – this death is still only the life of our minds. But the death of the sun is a death of mind, because it is the death of death as the life of the mind. There's no sublation or deferral if nothing survives. This annihilation is totally different from the one you harangue us about talking about 'our' death, a death that is part of the fate of living creatures who think. Annihilation in any case is too subjective. It will involve a change in the condition of matter: that is, in the form that energies take. This change is enough to render null and void your anticipation of a world after the explosion. Political science-fiction novels depict the cold desert of our human world after nuclear war. The solar explosion won't be due to human war. It won't leave behind it a devastated human world, dehumanized, but with none the less at least a single survivor, someone to tell the story of what's left, write it down. Dehumanized still implies human – a dead human, but conceivable: because dead in human terms, still capable of being sublated in thought. But in what remains after the solar explosion, there won't be any humanness, there won't be living creatures, there won't be intelligent, sensitive, sentient earthlings to bear witness to it, since they and their earthly horizon will have been consumed.

Assume that the ground, Husserl's *Ur-Erde*, will vanish into clouds of heat and matter. Considered as matter, the earth isn't at all originary since it's subject to changes in its condition – changes from further away or closer, changes coming from matter and energy and from the laws governing Earth's transformation. The *Erde* is an arrangement of matter/energy. This arrangement is transitory – lasting a few billion years more or less. Lunar years. Not a long time considered on a cosmic scale. The sun, our earth and your thought will have been no more than a spasmodic state of energy, an instant of established order, a smile on the surface of matter in a remote corner of the cosmos. You, the unbelievers, you're really believers: you believe much too much in that smile, in the complicity of things and thought,

10

in the purposefulness of all things! Like everyone else, you will end up victims of the stabilized relationships of order in that remote corner. You'll have been seduced and deceived by what you call nature, by a congruence of mind and things. Claudel called this a *'co-naissance'*, and Merleau-Ponty spoke of the chiasmus of the eye and the horizon, a fluid in which mind floats. The solar explosion, the mere thought of that explosion, should awaken you from this euphoria. Look here: you try to think of the event in its *quod*, in the advent of 'it so happens that' before any quiddity, don't you? Well, you'll grant the explosion of the sun is the *quod* itself, no subsequent assignment being possible. Of that death alone, Epicurus ought to have said what he says about death – that I have nothing to do with it, since if it's present, I'm not, and if I'm present, it's not. Human death is included in the life of human mind. Solar death implies an irreparably exclusive disjunction between death and thought: if there's death, then there's no thought. Negation without remainder. No self to make sense of it. Pure event. Disaster. All the events and disasters we're familiar with and try to think of will end up as no more than pale simulacra.

Now this event is ineluctable. So either you don't concern yourself with it – and remain in the life of the mind and in earthly phenomenality. Like Epicurus you say 'As long as it's not here, I am, and I continue philosophizing in the cozy lap of the complicity between man and nature.' But still with this glum afterthought: *après moi le déluge*. The deluge of matter. You'll grant there's a significant point of divergence between our thinking and the classical and modern thought of Western civilization: the obvious fact of there being no nature, but only the material monster of *D'Alembert's Dream*, the *chôra* of the *Timaeus*. Once we were considered able to converse with Nature. Matter asks no questions, expects no answers of us. It ignores us. It made us the way it made all bodies – by chance and according to its laws.

Or else you try to anticipate the disaster and fend it off with means belonging to that category – means that are those of the laws of the transformation of energy. You decide to accept the challenge of the extremely likely annihilation of a solar order and an order of your own thought. And then the

11

only job left you is quite clear – it's been underway for some time – the job of simulating conditions of life and thought to make thinking remain materially possible after the change in the condition of matter that's the disaster. This and this alone is what's at stake today in technical and scientific research in every field from dietetics, neurophysiology, genetics and tissue synthesis to particle physics, astrophysics, electronics, information science and nuclear physics. Whatever the immediate stakes might appear to be: health, war, production, communication. For the benefit of humankind, as the saying goes.

You know – technology wasn't invented by us humans. Rather the other way around. As anthropologists and biologists admit, even the simplest life forms, infusoria (tiny algae synthesized by light at the edges of tidepools a few million years ago) are already technical devices. Any material system is technological if it filters information useful to its survival, if it memorizes and processes that information and makes inferences based on the regulating effect of behaviour, that is, if it intervenes on and impacts its environment so as to assure its perpetuation at least. A human being isn't different in nature from an object of this type. Its equipment for absorbing data isn't exceptional compared to other living things. What's true is that this human being is omnivorous when dealing with information because it has a regulating system (codes and rules of processing) that's more differentiated and a storage capacity for its memory that's greater than those of other living things. Most of all: it's equipped with a symbolic system that's both arbitrary (in semantics and syntax), letting it be less dependent on an immediate environment, and also 'recursive' (Hofstadter), allowing it to take into account (above and beyond raw data) the way it has of processing such data. That is, itself. Hence, of processing as information its own rules in turn and of inferring other ways of processing information. A human, in short, is a living organization that is not only complex but, so to speak, replex. It can grasp itself as a medium (as in medicine) or as an organ (as in goal-directed activity) or as an object (as in thought – I mean aesthetic as well as speculative thought). It can even abstract itself from itself and take into account only its rules

12

of processing, as in logic and mathematics. The opposite limit of this symbolic recursiveness resides in the necessity by which it is bound (whatever its *meta*-level of operation) at the same time to maintain regulations that guarantee its survival in any environment whatsoever. Isn't that exactly what constitutes the basis of your transcendence in immanence? Now, until the present time, this environment has been terrestrial. The survival of a thinking-organization requires exchanges with that environment such that the human body can perpetuate itself there. This is equally true of the quintessential *meta*-function – philosophical thought. To think, at the very least you have to breathe, eat, etc. You are still under an obligation to 'earn a living'.

The body might be considered the hardware of the complex technical device that is human thought. If this body is not properly functioning, the ever so complex operations, the meta-regulations to the third or fourth power, the controlled deregulations of which you philosophers are so fond, are impossible. Your philosophy of the endless end, of immortal death, of interminable difference, of the undecidable, is an expression, perhaps the expression *par excellence*, of meta-regulation itself. It's as if it took itself into account as *meta*. Which is all well and good. But don't forget – this faculty of being able to change levels referentially derives solely from the symbolic and recursive power of language. Now language is simply the most complex form of the (living and dead) 'memories' that regulate all living things and make them technical objects better adjusted to their surroundings than mechanical ensembles. In other words your philosophy is possible only because the material ensemble called 'man' is endowed with very sophisticated software. But also, this software, human language, is dependent on the condition of the hardware. Now: the hardware will be consumed in the solar explosion taking philosophical thought with it (along with all other thought) as it goes up in flames.

So the problem of the technological sciences can be stated as: how to provide this software with a hardware that is independent of the conditions of life on earth.

That is: how to make thought without a body possible. A thought that continues to exist after the death of the human body. This is the price to be paid if the explosion is to be conceivable, if the death of the sun is to be a death like other deaths we know about. Thought without a body is the prerequisite for thinking of the death of all bodies, solar or terrestrial, and of the death of thoughts that are inseparable from those bodies.

But 'without a body' in this exact sense: without the complex living terrestrial organism known as the human body. Not without hardware, obviously.

So theoretically the solution is very simple: manufacture hardware capable of 'nurturing' software at least as complex (or replex) as the present-day human brain, but in non-terrestrial conditions. That clearly means finding for the 'body' envisaged a 'nutrient' that owes nothing to bio-chemical components synthesized on the surface of the earth through the use of solar energy. Or: learning to effect these syntheses in other places than on earth. In both cases then this means learning to manufacture a hardware capable of nourishing our software or its equivalent, but one maintained and supported only by sources of energy available in the cosmos generally.

It's clear even to a lay person like myself that the combined forces of nuclear physics, electronics, photonics and informa-tion science open up a possibility of constructing technical objects, with a capacity that's not just physical but also cognitive, which 'extract' (that is select, process and distrib-ute) energies these objects need in order to function from forms generally found everywhere in the cosmos.

So much for the hardware. As for the software such machines are to be equipped with – that's a subject for research in the area of artificial intelligence and for the controversies surrounding such research. You philosophers, writers and artists are quick to dismiss the pathetic track record of today's software programs. True – thinking or 'representing' machines (Monique Linard's term) are weak-lings compared to ordinary human brains, even untrained ones.

It can be objected that programmes fed into such comput-ers are elementary and that progress can be expected in information science, artificial languages and communications

14

science. Which is likely. But the main objection concerns the very principle of these intelligences. This objection has been summed up in a line of thought proposed by Hubert L. Dreyfus. Our disappointment in these organs of 'bodiless thought' comes from the fact that they operate on binary logic, one imposed on us by Russell's and Whitehead's mathematical logic, Turing's machine, McCulloch's and Pitts's neuronal model, the cybernetics of Wiener and von Neumann, Boolian algebra and Shannon's information science.

But as Dreyfus argues, human thought doesn't think in a binary mode. It doesn't work with units of information (bits), but with intuitive, hypothetical configurations. It accepts imprecise, ambiguous data that don't seem to be selected according to preestablished codes or readability. It doesn't neglect side effects or marginal aspects of a situation. It isn't just focused, but lateral too. Human thought can distinguish the important from the unimportant without doing exhaustive inventories of data and without testing the importance of data with respect to the goal pursued by a series of trials and errors. As Husserl has shown, thought becomes aware of a 'horizon', aims at a 'noema', a kind of object, a sort of non-conceptual monogram that provides it with intuitive configurations and opens up 'in front of it' a field of orientation and expectation, a 'frame' (Minsky). And in such a framework, perhaps more like a scheme, it moves towards what it looks for by 'choosing', that is, by discarding and recombining the data it needs, but none the less without making use of preestablished criteria determining in advance what's appropriate to choose. This picture inevitably recalls the description Kant gave of a thought process he called reflective judgement: a mode of thought not guided by rules for determining data, but showing itself as possibly capable of developing such rules afterwards on the basis of results obtained 'reflexively'.

This description of a reflective thought opposed to determinate thought does not hide (in the work of Husserl or Dreyfus) what it owes to perceptual experience. A field of thought exists in the same way that there's a field of vision (or hearing): the mind orients itself in it just as the eye does in

15

the field of the visible. In France, this analogy was already central to Wallon's work, for example, and also to Merleau-Ponty's. It is 'well known'. None the less it has to be stressed this analogy isn't extrinsic, but intrinsic. In its procedures it doesn't only describe a thought analogous with an experience of perception. It describes a thought that proceeds analogically and only analogically – not logically. A thought in which therefore procedures of the type – 'just as ... so likewise ...' or 'as if ... then' or again 'as p is to q, so r is to s' are privileged compared to digital procedures of the type 'if ... then ...' and 'p is not non-p.' Now these are the paradoxical operations that constitute the experience of a body, of an 'actual' or phenomenological body in its space-time continuum of sensibility and perception. Which is why it's appropriate to take the body as model in the manufacture and programming of artificial intelligence if it's intended that artificial intelligence not be limited to the ability to reason logically.

It's obvious from this objection that what makes thought and the body inseparable isn't just that the latter is the indispensable hardware for the former, a material prerequisite of its existence. It's that each of them is analogous to the other in its relationship with its respective (sensible, symbolic) environment: the relationship being analogical in both cases. In this description there are convincing grounds for not supporting the hypothesis (once suggested by Hilary Putnam) of a principle of the 'separability' of intelligence, a principle through which he believed he could legitimate an attempt to create artificial intelligence.

SHE

Now that's something to leave us satisfied as philosophers. At least something to assuage a part of our anxiety. A field of perception has limits, but these limits are always beyond reach. While a visual object is presenting one side to the eye, there are always other sides, still unseen. A direct, focused vision is always surrounded by a curved area where visibility is held in reserve yet isn't absent. This disjunction is

16

inclusive. And I'm not speaking of a memory brought into play by even the simplest sight. Continuing vision preserves along with it what was seen an instant before from another angle. It anticipates what will be seen shortly. These syntheses result in identifications of objects, identifications that never are completed, syntheses that a subsequent sighting can always unsettle or undo. And the eye, in this experience, is indeed always in search of a recognition, as the mind is of a complete description of an object it is trying to think of: without, however, a viewer ever being able to say he recognizes an object perfectly since the field of presentation is absolutely unique every time, and since when vision actually sees, it can't ever forget that there's always more to be seen once the object is 'identified'. Perceptual 'recognition' never satisfies the logical demand for complete description.

In any serious discussion of analogy it's this experience that is meant, this blur, this uncertainty, this faith in the inexhaustibility of the perceivable, and not just a mode of transfer of the data onto an inscription-surface not originally its own. Similarly, writing plunges into the field of phrases, moving forward by means of adumbrations, groping towards what it 'means' and never unaware, when it stops, that it's only suspending its exploration for a moment (a moment that might last a lifetime) and that there remains, beyond the writing that has stopped, an infinity of words, phrases and meanings in a latent state, held in abeyance, with as many things 'to be said' as at the beginning. Real 'analogy' requires a thinking or representing machine to be *in* its data *just as* the eye is in the visual field or writing is in language (in the broad sense). It isn't enough for these machines to simulate the results of vision or of writing fairly well. It's a matter (to use the attractively appropriate locution) of 'giving body' to the artificial thought of which they are capable. And it's that body, both 'natural' and artificial, that will have to be carried far from earth before its destruction if we want the thought that survives the solar explosion to be something more than a poor binarized ghost of what it was beforehand.

From this point of view we should indeed have grounds not to give up on techno-science. I have no idea whether such a 'programme' is achievable. Is it even consistent to claim to be

17

programming an experience that defies, if not programming, then at least the programme – as does the vision of the painter or writing? It's up to you to give it a try. After all, the problem's an urgent one for you. It's the problem of a comprehension of ordinary language by your machines. A problem you encounter especially in the area of terminal/user interface. In that interface subsists the contact of your artificial intelligence with the naive kind of intelligence borne by so-called 'natural' languages and immersed in them.

But another question bothers me. Is it really another question? Thinking and suffering overlap. Words, phrases in the act of writing, the latent nuances and timbres at the horizon of a painting or a musical composition as it's being created (you've said this yourselves) all lend themselves to us for the occasion and yet slip through our fingers. And even inscribed on a page or canvas, they 'say' something other than what we 'meant' because they're older than the present intent, overloaded with possibilities of meaning – that is, connected with other words, phrases, shades of meaning, timbres. By means of which precisely they constitute a field, a 'world', the 'brave' human world you were speaking about, but one that's probably more like an opaqueness of very distant horizons that exist only so that we'll 'brave' them. If you think you're describing thought when you describe a selecting and tabu-lating of data, you're silencing truth. Because data aren't given, but givable, and selection isn't choice. Thinking, like writing or painting, is almost no more than letting a givable come towards you. In the discussion we had last year at Siegen, in this regard, emphasis was put on the sort of emptiness that has to be obtained from mind and body by a Japanese warrior-artist when doing calligraphy, by an actor when acting: the kind of suspension of ordinary intentions of mind associated with *habitus*, or arrangements of the body. It's at this cost, said Glenn and Andreas (and you can imagine how quickly I agreed, helped out by Dôgen, Diderot and Kleist), that a brush encounters the 'right' shapes, that a voice and a theatrical gesture are endowed with the 'right' tone and look. This soliciting of emptiness, this evacuation – very much the opposite of overweening, selective, identificatory activity – doesn't take place without some suffering. I won't

18

claim that the grace Kleist talked about (a grace of stroke, tone or volume) has to be merited: that would be presumptuous of me. But it has to be called forth, evoked. The body and the mind have to be free of burdens for grace to touch us. That doesn't happen without suffering. An enjoyment of what we possessed is now lost.

Here again, you will note, there's a necessity for physical experience and a recourse to exemplary cases of bodily ascesis to understand and make understood a type of emptying of the mind, an emptying that is required if the mind is to think. This obviously has nothing to do with *tabula rasa*, with what Descartes (vainly) wanted to be a starting from scratch on the part of knowing thought – a starting that paradoxically can only be a starting all over again. In what we call thinking the mind isn't 'directed' but suspended. You don't give it rules. You teach it to receive. You don't clear the ground to build unobstructed: you make a little clearing where the penumbra of an almost-given will be able to enter and modify its contour. An example of this work is found *mutatis mutandis* in Freudian *Durcharbeitung*. In which – though I won't labour the point – the pain and the cost of the work of thought can be seen. This kind of thinking has little to do with combining symbols in accordance with a set of rules. Even though the act of combining, as it seeks out and waits for its rule, can have quite a lot to do with thought.

The pain of thinking isn't a symptom coming from outside to inscribe itself on the mind instead of in its true place. It is thought itself resolving to be irresolute, deciding to be patient, wanting not to want, wanting, precisely, not to produce a meaning in place of what *must* be signified. This is a tip of the hat to a *duty* that hasn't yet been named. Maybe that duty isn't a debt. Maybe it's just the mode according to which what doesn't yet exist, a word, a phrase, a colour, *will emerge*. So that the suffering of thinking is a suffering of time, of what happens. To sum up – will your thinking-, your representing-machines suffer? What will be their future if they are just memories? You will tell me this scarcely matters if at least they can 'achieve' the paradoxical relationship to the said 'data', which are only quasi-givens, givables, which I've just described. But this is a hardly credible proposition.

19

If this suffering is the mark of true thought, it's because we think in the already-thought, in the inscribed. And because it's difficult to leave something hanging in abeyance or take it up again in a different way so what hasn't been thought yet can emerge and what *should be* inscribed *will be*. I'm not speaking just about words lacking in a superabundance of available words, but about ways of assembling these words, ways we should accept despite the articulations inspired in us by logic, by the syntax of our languages, by constructions inherited from our reading. (To Sepp Gumbrecht, who was surprised that any and all thought, according to me, should require and involve inscription, I say: we think in a world of inscriptions already there. Call this culture if you like. And if we think, this is because there's still something missing in this plenitude and room has to be made for this lack by making the mind a blank, which allows the something else remaining to be thought to happen. But this can only 'emerge' as already inscribed in its turn.) The unthought hurts because we're comfortable in what's already thought. And thinking, which is accepting this discomfort, is also, to put it bluntly, an attempt to have done with it. That's the hope sustaining all writing (painting, etc.): that at the end, things will be better. As there is no end, this hope is illusory. So: the unthought would have to make your machines uncomfortable, the uninscribed that remains to be inscribed would have to make their memory suffer. Do you see what I mean? Otherwise why would they ever *start* thinking? We need machines that suffer from the burden of their memory. (But suffering doesn't have a good reputation in the technological megalopolis. Especially the suffering of thinking. It doesn't even incite laughter anymore. The idea of it doesn't occur, that's all. There's a trend towards 'play', if not performance.)

Finally, the human body has a gender. It's an accepted proposition that sexual difference is a paradigm of an incompleteness of not just bodies, but minds too. Of course there's masculinity in women as well as femininity in men. Otherwise how would one gender even have an idea of the other or have an emotion that comes from what's lacking? It's lacking because it's present deep inside, in the body, in the mind. Present like a guard, restrained, off to the side, at the

20

edge of your vision, present on some horizon of it. Elusive, impossible to grasp. Again we're back at transcendence in immanence. The notion of gender dominant in contemporary society wants this gap closed, this transcendence toppled, this powerlessness overcome. Supposed 'partners' (in a pleasure arrangement) draw up a contract for purposes of common 'enjoyment' of sexual difference itself. The contract provides that neither party suffer from this association and that at the first sign of lack (whether through failure to perform or not), of defocalization, of lack of control and transcendence, the parties break the contract – though that's still too strong a phrase, they'll just let it lapse. And even if from time to time fashion gives 'love' its place back among the inventory of objects that circulate, it's as a 'top of the line' sexual relationship, reserved for superstars and advertised as an enviable exception. I see in this arrangement a sign that techno-science conditions thought to neglect the different it carries within.

I don't know whether sexual difference is ontological difference. How would a person *know*? My unassuming phenomenological description still doesn't go far enough. Sexual difference isn't just related to a body as it feels its incompleteness, but to an unconscious body or to the unconscious as body. That is, as separated from thought – even analogical thought. This difference is *ex hypothesi* outside our control. Maybe (because as Freud showed in his description of deferred action, it inscribes effects without the inscription being 'memorized' in the form of recollection) it's the other way around? And this difference is what initially sets up fields of perception and thought as functions of waiting, of equivocations, as I've stated? This quite probably defines suffering in perceiving and conceiving as produced by an impossibility of unifying and completely determining the object seen. To that which without gendered difference would only be a neutral experience of the space-time of perceptions and thoughts, an experience in which this feeling of incompleteness would be lacking as unhappiness, but only an experience producing a simple and pure cognitive aesthetic, to this neutrality gendered difference adds the suffering of abandonment because it brings to neutrality what no field of

21

vision or thought can include, namely a demand. The faculty to transcend the given that you were talking about, a faculty lodged in immanence indeed finds a means to do this in the recursiveness of human language – although such a capacity isn't just a possibility but an actual force. And that force is desire.

So: the intelligence you're preparing to survive the solar explosion will have to carry that force within it on its interstellar voyage. Your thinking machines will have to be nourished not just on radiation but on the irremediable differend of gender.

And here is where the issue of complexity has to be brought up again. I'm granting to physics theory that technological-scientific development is, on the surface of the earth, the present-day form of a process of negentropy or complexification that has been underway since the earth began its existence. I'm granting that human beings aren't and never have been the motor of this complexification, but an effect and carrier of this negentropy, its continuer. I'm granting that the disembodied intelligence that everything here conspires to create will make it possible to meet the challenge to that process of complexification posed by an entropic tidal wave which from that standpoint equates with the solar explosion to come. I agree that with the cosmic exile of this intelligence a locus of high complexity – a centre of negentropy – will have escaped its most probable outcome, a fate promised any isolated system by Carnot's second law – precisely because this intelligence won't have let itself be left isolated in its terrestrial-solar condition. In granting all this, I concede that it isn't any human desire to know or transform reality that propels this techno-science, but a cosmic circumstance. But note that the complexity of that intelligence exceeds that of the most sophisticated logical systems, since it's another type of thing entirely. As a material ensemble, the human body hinders the separability of this intelligence, hinders its exile and therefore survival. But at the same time the body, our phenomenological, mortal, perceiving body is the only available *analogon* for thinking a certain complexity of thought.

Thought makes lavish use of analogy. It does this in scientific discovery too of course 'before' its operativity is

22

fixed in paradigms. On the other hand its analogizing power can also return, bringing into play the spontaneous analogical field of the perceiving body, educating Cézanne's eye, Debussy's ear, to see and hear givables, nuances, timbres that are 'useless' for survival, even cultural survival.

But once again that analogizing power, which belongs to body and mind analogically and mutually and which body and mind share with each other in the art of invention, is inconsequential compared to an irreparable transcendence inscribed on the body by gender difference. Not only calculation, but even analogy cannot do away with the remainder left by this difference. This difference makes thought go on endlessly and won't allow itself to be thought. Thought is inseparable from the phenomenological body: although gendered body is separated from thought, and launches thought. I'm tempted to see in this difference a primordial explosion, a challenge to thought that's comparable to the solar catastrophe. But such is not the case, since this difference causes infinite thought – held as it is in reserve in the secrecy of bodies and thoughts. It annihilates only the One. You have to prepare post-solar thought for the inevitability and complexity of this separation. Or the pilot at the helm of spaceship *Exodus* will still be entropy.

2

Rewriting Modernity

The title 'rewriting modernity' was suggested to me by Kathy Woodward and Carol Teneson of the Center of 20th Century Studies in Milwaukee. I thank them for it: it seems far preferable to the usual headings, like 'postmodernity', 'postmodernism', 'postmodern', under which this sort of reflection is usually placed. The advantage of 'rewriting modernity' depends on two displacements: the transformation of the prefix 'post-' into 're-' from the lexical point of view, and the syntactical application of this modified prefix to the verb 'writing', rather than to the substantive 'modernity'.

This double displacement points to two main directions. First of all it shows up the pointlessness of any periodization of cultural history in terms of 'pre-' and 'post-', before and after, for the single reason that it leaves unquestioned the position of the 'now', of the present from which one is supposed to be able to achieve a legitimate perspective on a chronological succession. For the old 'continental' philosopher I am, this effect cannot fail to recall Aristotle's analysis of time in Book IV of the *Physics*. The substance of what he says is that it is impossible to determine the difference between what has taken place (the *proteron*, the anterior) and what comes along (the *husteron*, the ulterior) without situating the flux of events with respect to a now. But it is no less impossible to grasp any such *'now'* since, because it is dragged away by what we call the flow of consciousness, the course of life, of things, of events, whatever – it never stops fading

24

away. So that it is always both too soon and too late to grasp anything like a 'now' in an identifiable way. The 'too late' signifies an excess in the 'going away', disappearing, the 'too early' an excess in advent. An excess with respect to what? To the intention to identify, the project of seizing and identifying an 'entity' that would, 'here and now', be the thing itself.

When this argument is applied to modernity, the result is that neither modernity nor so-called postmodernity can be identified and defined as clearly circumscribed historical entities, of which the latter would always come 'after' the former. Rather we have to say that the postmodern is always implied in the modern because of the fact that modernity, modern temporality, comprises in itself an impulsion to exceed itself into a state other than itself. And not only to exceed itself in that way, but to resolve itself into a sort of ultimate stability, such for example as is aimed at by the utopian project, but also by the straightforward political project implied in the grand narratives of emancipation. Modernity is constitutionally and ceaselessly pregnant with its postmodernity.

Rather than the postmodern, what would be properly opposed to modernity here would be the classical age. The classical age involves a state of time (let's call it a status of temporality) in which advent and passing, future and past, are treated as though, taken together, they embraced the totality of life in one and the same unity of meaning. For example, this would be the way that myth organizes and distributes time, creating a rhythm of the beginning and end of the story it recounts, to the point of making them rhyme.

From this same point of view, we can see that historical periodization belongs to an obsession that is characteristic of modernity. Periodization is a way of placing events in a diachrony, and diachrony is ruled by the principle of revolution. In the same way that modernity contains the promise of its overcoming, it is obliged to mark, to date, the end of one period and the beginning of the next. Since one is inaugurating an age reputed to the entirely new, it is right to set the clock to the new time, to start it from zero again. In Christianity, Cartesianism or Jacobinism, this same gesture designates a Year One, that of revelation and redemption in

25

the one case, of rebirth and renewal in the second, or again of revolution and reappropriation of liberties.

These three figures of the 're-' herald an essential aspect of the question of rewriting – the second of the two I noted at the beginning. The ambiguity of the term 'rewriting' is the very same ambiguity that haunts the relation of modernity with time. Rewriting can consist in the gesture I've just mentioned of starting the clock again from zero, wiping the slate clean, the gesture which inaugurates in one go the beginning of the new age and the new periodization. The use of the 're-' means a return to the starting point, to a beginning that is supposed to be exempt from any prejudice because it is imagined that prejudices result solely from the stocking up and tradition of judgements that were previously held to be true without having reconsidered them. The game that is then played between the 'pre-' and the 're-' (taken in the sense of a return) aims to erase the 'pre-' implied in some at least of these old judgements. For example, this is how we must take the name 'prehistory' given by Marx to any human history preceding the socialist revolution he is expecting and preparing.

We can now clarify a second and quite different sense of this 're-'. Essentially linked with writing in this sense, the 're-' in no way signifies a return to the beginning but rather what Freud called a 'working through', *Durcharbeitung*, i.e. a working attached to a thought of what is constitutively hidden from us in the event and the meaning of the event, hidden not merely by past prejudice, but also by those dimensions of the future marked by the pro-ject, the pro-grammed, pro-spectives, and even by the pro-position and the pro-posal to psychoanalyze.

In a short but – if I may say so – memorable text bearing on psychoanalytic 'technique', Freud distinguishes repetition, remembering and working through. Repetition, which is the business of neurosis or psychosis, is the result of a 'set-up' which allows the unconscious desire to be fulfilled and which organizes the whole existence of the subject like a drama. The life of the patient subject to desire thus set up would take the form of a fate or destiny. The story of Oedipus provided Freud with his model for this. In destiny, the beginning and

26

end of the story rhyme with one another, and this is how this story comes under the organization of time I called 'classical', in which the gods – the god, as Hölderlin says – never stop intervening. The set-up of desire formulated by the oracle of Apollo establishes in advance the major events that Oedipus will encounter in the course of his story. The life of the king is, as it were, stamped, his future inscribed in the past already said, the *fatum* of which he is ignorant, and which he therefore repeats.

But things are not as simple as I'm suggesting. In both Sophocles's tragedy and in Freud's analysis, Oedipus, or the patient, tries to bring to consciousness, to discover the 'reason' or the 'cause' of the trouble s/he suffers and has suffered all his or her life. S/he wants to remember, to gather up the dismembered temporality that has not been mastered. Childhood is the name borne by this lost time. So King Oedipus starts searching for the cause of the evil, a sin that would be at the origin of the plague the city is suffering. The patient on the couch appears to be involved in an entirely similar enquiry. Like in a detective novel, the case is examined, witnesses called, information gathered. And so what I would call a second-order plot is woven, which deploys its own story above the plot in which is destiny is fulfilled, and whose aim is to remedy that destiny.

It is frequently the case that 'rewriting modernity' is understood in this sense, the sense of remembering, as though the point were to identify crimes, sins, calamities engendered by the modern set-up – and in the end to reveal the destiny that an oracle at the beginning of modernity would have prepared and fulfilled in our history.

We know how misleading in its turn rewriting thus understood can be. The trap resides in the fact that the enquiry into the origins of destiny is itself part of that destiny, and that the question of the beginning of the plot is posed at the end of the plot because it merely constitutes its end. The hero then becomes the culprit as the detective unmasks him. And this is why there is no 'perfect crime', no crime that could remain unknown forever. A secret would not be a 'real' secret if no-one knew it was a secret. For the crime to be prefect, it would have to be known to be perfect, and by that very fact it stops being perfect. To make the point differently, but within the same order of memory, à la John Cage, there is no silence that is not heard as such, and therefore makes some noise. Basically the same plot weaves an intimacy between silence and sound, criminal and cop, unconscious and consciousness.

If we understand 'rewriting modernity' in this way, like seeking out, designating and naming the hidden facts that one imagines to be the source of the ills that ail one, i.e. as a simple process of remembering, one cannot fail to perpetuate the crime, and perpetrate it anew instead of putting an end to it. Far from really rewriting it, supposing that to be possible, all one is doing is writing again, and making real, modernity itself. The point being that writing it is always rewriting it. Modernity is written, inscribes itself on itself, in a perpetual rewriting.

Let me illustrate this trap with two examples. Marx detects the hidden functioning of capitalism. At the heart of the process of emancipation and the coming to consciousness he places the disalienation of labour-power. In this way he believes he has identified and denounced the original crime from which is born the unhappiness of modernity: the exploitation of the workers. And like a detective, he imagines that by revealing 'reality' – i.e. liberal society and economics – as a fraud, he is allowing humanity to escape its great plague. Today we know that the October Revolution only succeeded, under the aegis of Marxism, and that any revolution only does and will succeed, in opening the same wound again. The localization and diagnosis may change, but the same illness re-emerges in this rewriting. Marxists believed that they worked to disalienate humanity, but the alienation of man has been repeated in scarcely displaced form.

And now from philosophy. Nietzsche tries to emancipate thought, the way of thinking, from what he calls metaphysics, i.e. from that principle, prevalent from Plato to Schopenhauer, which states that the only thing is for humans to discover the ground which will allow them to speak in accordance with the true and to act in accordance with the good or the just. The central theme of Nietzsche's thought is that there is no 'in accordance with', because there is nothing

28

that is a primary or originary principle, a *Grund*, as the Idea of the Good was for Plato or, for Leibniz, the principle of sufficient reason. Every discourse, including that of science or philosophy, is only a perspective, a *Weltanschauung*.

But at just that point Nietzsche succumbs to the temptation to designate what grounds the perspectivizations, and calls it the will to power. His philosophy thus reiterates the metaphysical process, and even obstinately and repetitively accomplishes its essence, for the metaphysics of will with which he concludes his enquiry is the very metaphysics harboured by all the philosophical systems of modern Western thought, as Heidegger shows.

The fact that Nietzsche's rewriting repeats the same error or fault in spite of itself is a sign for reflection of what a rewriting could be that escaped, as far as possible, the repetition of what it rewrites. It could be that the mainspring of the process of remembering was will itself. This is what Freud glimpses when he dissociates *Durcharbeitung*, working through, from remembering, *Errinerung*.

Remembering, one still *wants* too much. One wants to get hold of the past, grasp what has gone away, master, exhibit the initial crime, the lost crime of the origin, show it as such as though it could be disentangled from its affective context, the connotations of fault, of shame, of pride, of anguish in which we are still plunged at present, and which are precisely what motivate the idea of an origin.

By endeavouring to find an objectively first cause, like Oedipus, one forgets that the very will to identify the origin of the evil is made necessary by desire. For it is of the essence of desire to desire also to free itself of itself, because desire is intolerable. So one believes one can put an end to desire, and one fulfils its end (this is the ambiguity of the word *end*, aim and cessation: the same ambiguity as with desire). One tries to remember, and this is probably a good way of forgetting again.

If it is true that historical knowledge demands that its object be isolated and withdrawn from any libidinal investment come from the historian, then it is certain that the only result of this way of 'putting down' [*rédiger*] history would be to 'put it down' [*réduire*]. I'm invoking here the two meanings

29

said simultaneously by the Latin *redigere* and the English 'putting down' – to write down and to repress. Just as the English *writing down* suggests both inscription or recording and discredit. This type of rewriting can be found in many a history text, and it is this that Nietzsche is aiming at in the *Untimely Meditations* when questioning the trap at work in historical research.

And it is doubtless an awareness of this trap, again, that leads Freud finally to give up his hypothesis on the origin of the neuroses. He first attributed it to what he calls a 'primal scene', a scene of seduction of the child by the adult. By abandoning the realism of the beginning, Freud opens himself, on the older side psychoanalysis, its end, to the idea that the process of the cure could be, must be, interminable. Contrary to remembering, working through would be defined as a work without end and therefore without will: without end in the sense in which it is not guided by the concept of an end – but not without finality.

No doubt the most pertinent conception we can have of rewriting resides in this double gesture, forwards and backwards. We know that Freud especially stresses the rule of so-called 'freely floating attention' which the analyst is to observe with respect to the patient. It consists in according the same attention to every element of the sentences proffered by the analysand, however tiny and futile it may appear.

Basically, the rule states: do not prejudge, suspend judgement, give the same attention to everything that happens as it happens. On his or her side the patient must respect the symmetrical rule: let speech run, give free rein to all the 'ideas', figures, scenes, names, sentences, as they come onto the tongue and the body, in their 'disorder', without selection or repression.

A rule of this sort obliges the mind to be 'patient', in a new sense: no longer that of passively and repetitively enduring the same ancient and actual passion, but of applying its own passibility, a same respondent or 'respons', to everything that comes upon the mind, to give itself as a passage to the events which come to it from a 'something' that it does not know. Freud calls this attitude 'free association'. All it is is a way of linking one sentence with another without regard for the logical, ethical or aesthetic value of the link.

You will ask me what relation this practice can have with rewriting modernity. I recall that in working through, the only guiding thread at one's disposal consists in sentiment or, better, in listening to a sentiment. A fragment of a sentence, a scrap of information, a word, come along. They are immediately linked with another 'unit'. No reasoning , no argument, no mediation. By proceeding in this way, one slowly approaches a scene, the scene of something. One describes it. One does not know what it is. One is sure only that it refers to some past, both furthest and nearest past, both one's own past and others' past. This lost time is not represented like in a picture, it is not even presented. It is what presents the elements of a picture, an impossible picture. Rewriting means registering these elements.

It is clear that this rewriting provides no knowledge of the past. This is what Freud thinks too. Analysis is not subject to knowledge, but to 'technique', art. The result is not the definition of a past element. On the contrary, it presupposes that the past itself is the actor or agent that gives to the mind the elements with which the scene will be constructed.

But this scene in its turn in no way claims faithfully to represent the supposed 'primal scene'. It is 'new' in so far as it is felt as new. One can say of what has gone that it is there, alive, lively. Not present like an object, if an object can ever be present, but present like an *aura*, a gentle breeze, an allusion. Proust's *Recherche*, Benjamin's *One-way Street* or *Berlin Childhood* operate according to this same *techne* (obviously without being reducible to it). And at risk of seeming weird, I'd add that the procedure of freely and equally floating attention is what is at work in Montaigne's *Essais*.

Three observations, by way of an impossible conclusion. First, even if Freud did come to think that this 'technique' was an art, as the Greek *techne* says, he none the less did not lose sight of the fact that it was inscribed as a constitutive element in a process of emancipation. Thanks to it, the point is to deconstruct the rhetoric of the unconscious, the preorganized sets of signifiers that constitute the neurotic or

31

psychotic set-up and which organize the subject's life as a destiny. This does not seem to me to be the right hypothesis. In describing very briefly what I meant by rewriting, I had in mind an idea I cannot develop here. I shall simply point out how close that description of rewriting is to Kant's analysis of the work of the imagination in taste, in the pleasure in the beautiful. Both give the same importance to the freedom with which the elements provided by sensibility are treated, and both insist on the fact that the forms in play in pure aesthetic pleasure or in free association and listening are as independent as can be from any empirical or cognitive interest. The beauty of the phenomenon is in proportion to its fluidity, its mobility and its evanescence. Kant illustrates this with two metaphors, that of the ungraspable flame of a flaring in the hearth, and that of the evanescent design traced by the running water of a stream. And Kant comes round to concluding that the imagination gives the mind 'a lot to think', a lot more than does the conceptual work of the understanding. You see that this thesis is related to the question of time I posed at the beginning – the aesthetic grasp of forms is only possible if one gives up all pretension to master time through a conceptual synthesis. For what is in play here is not the 'recognition' of the given, as Kant says, but the ability to let things come as they present themselves. Following that sort of attitude, every moment, every now is an 'opening oneself to'. In support of this, I'd invoke Theodor Adorno or Ernst Bloch, and in particular the latter's *Spuren*. At the end of *Negative Dialectics*, and also in the unfinished *Aesthetic Theory*, Adorno lets it be understood that indeed we must rewrite modernity, that modernity is, moreover, its own rewriting, but that one can only rewrite it in the form of what he calls 'micrologies', which is not unrelated to Benjamin's 'passages'.

I have just stressed the features common to the free play of the aesthetic imagination and the free association or attention in play in the analytic relation. Of course we must also point out the heterogeneity. I'll list the essential differences to keep it short.

First, the pleasure procured by the beautiful is not the object of research, it happens or it doesn't, even if the artist

32

is aiming for it in the work. The artist is never master of this effect of taste. Aesthetic pleasure 'befalls' the mind like grace, an 'inspiration'. By contrast, the patient's discourse or the analyst's listening is work, working through, 'free' in its means, but called by an end. This end is of course not knowledge, but the approach to a 'truth' or a 'real' which is ungraspable.

And if this is so, then it means, secondly, that analytic work is motivated by an intolerable suffering which places the subject in a state of separation from itself, at the same time as this state sustains that same suffering in a repetitive way. It would be false to imagine that the cure could end on a reconciliation of consciousness with the unconscious. It is interminable because the dispossession of the subject, its subjection to a heteronomy, is constitutive for it. What there is of the *infans* in it, unsuited to proffering, is irreducible. By contrast, the pleasure in the beautiful is, as Stendhal and Adorno write, a 'promise of happiness' or, as Kant puts it, the promise of a sentimental community, *sensus communis*, of the subject with itself and also with others.

And finally, just as there is an aesthetic of the sublime which comes about through the distension of beautiful forms to the point of 'formlessness' (Kant) and which, from that very fact, brings about the overturning, the destruction, of the aesthetics of the beautiful, so according to Freud we must dissociate secondary repression (which gives rise to the 'formations' of the dream, the symptom, the parapraxis, etc., all the representations of the unconscious on the edges of the conscious scene) from what Lacan called the Thing, and Freud the unconscious affect, which never let themselves be presented. Primary repression, tightly connected with this Thing, would thus be to secondary repression what the sublime is to the beautiful.

Rewriting, as I mean it here, obviously concerns the anamnesis of the Thing. Not only that Thing that starts off a supposedly 'individual' singularity, but of the Thing that haunts the 'language', the tradition and the material with, against and in which one writes. In this way rewriting comes under a problematic of the sublime as much as, and today more than, more obviously than, a problematic of the

beautiful. Which opens right up the question of the relationship between aesthetics and ethics.

My second concluding observation is extremely simple.
What I've here called rewriting clearly has nothing to do with
what is called postmodernity or postmodernism on the
market of contemporary ideologies. This has nothing to do
with the use of parodies or quotations of modern or
modernist works as we can see it happening in architecture,
painting or theatre. And still less with the movement in
literature which is returning to the most traditional forms of
narrative. Forms and contents. I have myself used the term
'postmodern'. It was a slightly provocative way of placing (or
displacing) into the limelight the debate about knowledge.
Postmodernity is not a new age, but the rewriting of some of
the features claimed by modernity, and first of all modernity's
claim to ground its legitimacy on the project of liberating
humanity as a whole through science and technology. But as
I have said, that rewriting has been at work, for a long time
now, in modernity itself.

My last observation concerns the questions born of the
spectacular introduction of what are called the new technologies into the production, diffusion, distribution and consumption of cultural commodities. Why mention the fact
here? Because they are in the process of transforming culture
into an industry. A banal observation. One can also understand this change as a rewriting. The word is used in the
jargon of journalism, referring to an already ancient craft,
which consists in erasing all traces left in a text by unexpected
and 'fantasy' associations. The new technologies have given
that craft a considerable impetus, since they submit to exact
calculation every inscription on whatever support: visual and
sound images, speech, musical lines, and finally writing itself.
In my view, the noteworthy result of this is not, as
Baudrillard thinks, the constitution of an immense network
of simulacra. It seems to me that what is really disturbing is
much more the importance assumed by the concept of the *bit*,
the unit of information. When we're dealing with bits, there's
no longer any question of free forms given here and now to
sensibility and the imagination. On the contrary, they are
units of information conceived by computer engineering and

definable at all linguistic levels – lexical, syntactic, rhetorical and the rest. They are assembled into systems following a set of possiblities (a 'menu') under the control of a programmer. So that the question posed by the new technologies to the idea of rewriting as expressed here could be: it being admitted that working through is above all the business of free imagination and that it demands the deployment of time between 'not yet', 'no longer' and 'now', what can the use of the new technologies preserve or conserve of that? How can it still withdraw from the law of the concept, of recognition and prediction? For the moment, I shall content myself with the following reply: rewriting means resisting the writing of that supposed postmodernity.

3

Matter and Time

One of the questions posed is that of the use of the concept of matter in contemporary philosophy. What does the question mean? What is 'use of a concept'? Is a concept a tool? And then use to what purpose?

I see in the question the predominance of a technologistic thinking of thinking, i.e. a thinking of thinking as work. A mechanical energy, potential and/or kinetic, is applied to an object so as to transform it (movement in space; qualitative modification: *alloiôis*): 'productive' use.

Now such an object is called in dynamics a material point or system.

With matter come force, and the different sorts of energy, and work.

Are these metaphors? Or else is it thus that what we still call thought operates? An energy applied to a material point so as to transform it? With in that case the 'concept' playing the role of transformer?

There are several families of transformers because there are several forms taken by energy: mechanical, calorific, electrical, chemical, rays, nuclear. Should we add thinking or spiritual energy, as Bergson used to put it?

The 'material points' to which each of these forms of energy is applied are all different. Cartesian mechanics studies 'bodies' which are perceptible to human observation and transformations analogical to human experience.

36

The transformation of elements, such as the transformation of uranium 238 into neptunium, by bombarding the nuclei with neutrons, are not only not on our scale, but require an idea of matter of which the philosopher, ignorant and timid as he is, notes at least this – that it seems no longer to give any credence to the substance model.

I

Cartesian mechanics, and metaphysics, need no more than a naked substance. 'The nature of matter or of the body taken in general does not consist in its being a hard, or heavy, or coloured thing, or which touches our senses in some other way, but only in that it is a substance extended in length, breadth and depth' (*Principles of Philosophy*, II, 4). Such is the body, 'substance of material things'. Extension is infinitely divisible (§20), and thus is not constituted of simple elements (atoms), contains no void (§16–18), is homogeneous and continuous; it is indefinite (§21).

A body in the narrow sense is a part of extension. Movement is the changing of place of this body, from one bodily neighbourhood to another. The movement is only relative to an observer judged to be immobile. So that there is no substantial difference between rest and movement. Movement does not demand any particular form, it is a property of the mobile, and rest is another property of it. Mechanics is a part of geometry, study and production of figures in movement. The only relevant transformers are the axioms of classic geometry. Cartesian matter is a concept – extension – which is perfectly transparent to geometrico-algebraic thought. Everything that comes to us from it via the senses is removed from it as appearance. As my body is a part of extension, it cannot inform me about extension in general and its mathematical logic. Physiology, to the contrary, attempts to explain appearances (hardness, weight, colour, etc.) by the mechanism of figures and movements alone. The machine has to be rediscovered under the sensibility which is no more than a theatrical effect of it.

We would say today that there is no matter in Cartesian thought. The foreclosure of the 'material other' inspires the decision to deny the 'knowledges' of the body proper. The union of soul and body remains an intractable enigma. The soul unites only with itself, via its own transformers, innate ideas, the categories.

The soul has at its disposal the only language. The body is a confused speaker: it says 'soft', 'warm', 'blue', 'heavy', instead of talking straight lines, curves, collisions and relations.

Matter thus denied, foreclosed, remains present in this violently modern thinking: it is the enigmatic confusion of the past, the confusion of the badly built city, of childhood, ignorant and blind, of the cross-eyed look of the little girl loved by René Descartes as a child. Of everything that comes to us from behind, 'before'. Confusion, prejudice, is matter in thought, the disorder of the past which takes place before having been wanted and conceived, which does not know what it is saying, which must be endlessly translated and corrected, currently and actively, into distinct intuitions. Childhood, the unconscious, time, because 'then' is 'now', the old, are the matter that the understanding claims to resolve in the act and actuality of the instantaneous *intuitus*.

All energy belongs to the thinking that says what it says, wants what it wants. Matter is the failure of thought, its inert mass, stupidity.

We say: what impatience, what anguish in Cartesian modernism!

II

Nuclear transformations such as those which affect certain material elements known as radioactive, or those which take place in those transmutation-crucibles we call stars, or those which we provoke by bombarding and fission of the nucleus of plutonium or uranium 235 – such transformations not only required the long history of physics research from Descartes to Heisenberg, they also presuppose a complete overturning of the image of matter. And it is against this overturned image, however confused it may be for a mind as ill-informed as mine, that contemporary thought is inevitably measured, closely or at a distance.

One essential feature of this overturning of the image of matter consists in the preeminence of time in the analysis of the relation of body to mind. 'The questions relative to subject and object, their distinction and their union must be posed in terms of time rather than space', writes Bergson (*Matière et mémoire*, §4). The author of *L'énergie spirituelle* recalls this sentence of Leibniz's: 'One can consider every body as a mind that is instantaneous but deprived of memory' (Letter to Arnauld, November 1671).

The instant which in Descartes marked the spiritual act, which was the timeless time of the understanding, here swings over to the side of material actuality. The bare monad forgets itself from one moment to the next. True mind is memory and anamnesis, continuous time. None the less, this memory remains local, limited to a 'point to view'. God alone has or is the memory of the whole, and of its programme. He alone has at his disposal all the 'notions' of the monads, of all the properties they develop, have developed, and will develop. Absolute memory, which is at the same time timeless act. The localization of the created monads is the spatial version of their temporality. They have a 'point of view' immanent to space because they are immanent to time, because they do not have enough memory, because they do not gather themselves sufficiently together.

Considered spatially, every monad is a material point in interaction (direct interaction in Bergson, in Leibniz mediated by divine wisdom, which ensures the harmony of all the interactions) with all the other material points. This is why Bergson can call this material point an 'image' (in *Matière et mémoire*), and why Leibniz endows it with a 'perception'. The whole world is reflected in each material point, but what is the furthest from it, which thus takes the longest time to be made distinct (as one counts distances in temporal terms in mountain walks or interstellar expeditions), can only be inscribed on the 'mirror' if the material point has the capacity to assemble and conserve a lot of information at once, as we would say. Otherwise, the recording can certainly take place but remains unknown. So we must imagine that from matter to mind there is but a differences of degree, which depends on the capacity to gather and conserve. Mind is matter which remembers its interactions, its immanence. But there is a continuum from the instantaneous mind of matter to the very gathered matter of minds.

If there is such a continuity between the states of matter, this is because all material unities, even the 'barest', as is said in the *Monadology*, can only consist in their form, as Aristotle had understood it. For matter considered as 'mass' is infinitely divisible, and the unity it can produce is only phenomenal. This is the case with each human body, which doesn't stop changing in its mass, and has real and exact unity only through its difference, its 'point of view', itself determined by its 'form', i.e. its ability to gather up the actions exerted upon it (what we're calling interactions). If there are 'atoms of substance', these are therefore 'metaphysical points'; 'they have something vital and a sort of perception, and mathematical points are their point of view, to express the universe', in the words of the *Système nouveau de la nature.*

This quasi-perception – which makes me think so strongly of the 'pre-reflexive cogito' that Merleau-Ponty tried to isolate, or of the 'pure perception', perfect coextension of perceived and perceiver hypothesized by Bergson at the beginning of *Matière et mémoire* (I'll come back to this) – is none other than the '*expression* in a single indivisible being of divisible phenomena or of several beings', writes Leibniz to Arnauld (about 1688–90). No need, he adds, 'to attach thought or reflection to this representation': the perception can remain unperceived. And it must be shown that there are these 'material expressions which are without thought' not only in animals, but in living creatures such as vegetables, and even in 'bodily substances', writes Leibniz.

So I imagine this formal atom as the point at which all the images the monad has of the universe come to be projected. None of them has the whole of the universe in its mirror (*Monadology*, §56), otherwise it would be indiscernible from another monad. Now a *being* is *a* being. In matter, it is not the 'mass' which obeys the principle of the identity of indiscernibles – on the contrary, it is a crowd – but rather the form, which is the projection onto a mathematical point of a texture of relations. And if the images change on the mirror of each formal atom, then all the other mirrors must reflect, each according to its point of view, the complementary changes of the first. This harmony is ensured by divine wisdom, alone in representing everything, whilst the differentiation of the 'points of view', the multiplication of the monads, which causes the diversity of the world and the complexity of bodies, is a result of the principle that the all-powerful must deploy all its possibilities.

Our laicized science calls that 'all-power' energy, and it refers the responsibility for the convergence between the points of matter, their compossibility, not to a wisdom, but to chance and to selection, which 'fix' (for immensely differing 'lifetimes') material organizations, 'formal atoms', always precarious.

III

I return for a moment to the 'pure perception' imagined by Bergson in *Matière et mémoire*, to bring out how Leibnizian in principle is his problematic of the relation between matter and mind. Of course, the working hypothesis is entirely different – pragmatic, if you like: the living body is an agent of the transformation of things, all perception induces an action. But what is not pragmatist is that this term 'perception' is applied by Bergson to every material point: 'The more the reaction must be immediate, the more the perception must resemble a simple contact, and the complete process of perception and reaction must be scarcely distinct from a mechanical impulse followed by a necessary movement' (*Matière et mémoire*, p. 28).

The further one climbs the ladder of organized beings, the more one observes that the immediate reaction is delayed, 'prevented', and that this inhibition explains the indeterminacy, unpredictability and growing freedom of the actions these beings can perform.

Bergson sees the reason for this inhibition in the extension and complexity of the nervous relays interposed between the afferent or sensitive fibres and the efferent or motor fibres. The 'mirror' gets more complicated, and the influx on its way out can be filtered down many paths.

It will only go down one of them – and this will be that of the real action performed. But many other actions were possible and will remain inscribed in a virtual state. This is how perception stops being 'pure', i.e. instantaneous, and how representational consciousness can be born of this reflection (in the optical sense), of this 'echo', of the influx on the set of other possible – but currently ignored – paths which form memory. (And even then we are only talking about immediate memory or habit. Recollection [*souvenir*] will be the memory of that memory.) This is how what is given one by one, blow by blow, or, as Bergson puts it, 'shock' [*ébranlement*] by shock, in the amnesiac material point, is 'retracted', condensed as though into a single high-frequency vibration, in perception aided by memory. The relevant different between mind and matter is one of rhythm. In an 'instant' of conscious perception, which is in fact an indivisible block of duration made of vibration, 'memory condenses an enormous multiplicity of shocks, which appear simultaneously to us although they are successive' (*Matière et mémoire*, p. 73). In order to get back to matter from a consciousness, it would suffice to 'divide ideally this undivided thickness of time, and distinguish in it the desired multiplicity of movements' (ibid.).

Let us take as an example one of the those 'secondary qualities' abandoned by the mechanisitic explanation, the colour red. Science which takes this as real matter sees in red light a vibration of the electro-magnetic field at a frequency, according to Bergson, of 400 trillion vibrations per second. The human eye needs two thousandths of a second to make a temporal dissociation between two pieces of information. If it had to dissociate the vibrations condensed in the perception of red, it would take 25,000 years. But if it synchronized itself to that rhythm, it would no longer perceive red at all, and would, says Bergson, register only 'pure shocks', since it would be coextensive with them. It would be, instant by instant, each of those shocks itself. It would be a 'pure' or 'bare' material point.

IV

The continuity between mind and matter thus appears as a particular case of the transformation of frequencies into other frequencies, and this is what the transformation of energy consists in. Contemporary science, I believe, shows us that energy, in all its forms, is distributed in waves, and that, to quote Jean Perrin, 'all matter is in the end a particular and very condensed form of energy.' The reality to be accorded to such-and-such a form of energy, and therefore of matter, clearly depends on the transformers we have at our disposal. Even the transformer that our central nervous system is, highly sophisticated in the order of living creatures, can only transcribe and inscribe according to its own rhythm the excitations which come to it from the milieu in which it lives.

If we have at our disposal interfaces capable of memorizing, in a fashion accessible to us, vibrations naturally beyond our ken, i.e. that determine us as no more than 'material points' (as is the case with many forms of radiation), then we are extending our power of differentiation and our memories, we are delaying reactions which are as yet not under control, we are increasing our material liberty. This complex of transformers, still seen from the pragmatist point of view, well deserves the name it bears, that of techno-science.

The new technologies, built on electronics and data processing, must be considered – still from the same angle – as material extensions of our capacity to memorize, more in Leibniz's sense that Bergson's, given the role played in them by symbolic language as supreme 'condenser' of all information. These technologies show in their own way that there is no break between matter and mind, at least in its reactive functions, which we call performance-functions. They have a cortex, or a cortex-element, which has the property of being collective, precisely because it is physical and not biological. Which cannot but raise some questions which I shall not address here.

I should like instead to end by trying to respond to our initial question: what impact can the idea of matter I've just broadly summarized have on philososphy?

It is possible to give a pragmatic turn to a philosophy of matter, as does Bergson in *Matière et mémoire*, which then – whatever Bergson may have thought about it – can easily be linked with the ambiant technologism or techno-scientism. The link of the one philosophy with the other does, however, demand a correction, which on reflection is no mere detail, and of which Bergson was perfectly aware. Pragmatism, as its name suggests, is one of the many versions of humanism. The human subject it presupposes is, to be sure, material, involved in a *milieu*, and turned towards action. The fact remains that this action is given a finality by an interest, which is represented as a sort of optimum adjustment of subject to environment. But if one looks at the history of the sciences and techniques (and of the arts, of which I have said nothing, even though the question of matter, of material especially, is decisive for them), one notices that this was not, and is not – especially today – in fact their finality.

The complexification of the transformers, theoretical and practical, has always had as its effect the destabilization of the fit between the human subject and its environment. And it always modifies this fit in the same direction – it delays reaction, it increases possible responses, increases material liberty and, in this sense, can only disappoint the demand for security which is inscribed in the human being as in every living organism. In other words, it does not seem that the desire – let's call it that – to complexify memory can come under the demand for equilibrium in the relation of man with his milieu. Pragmatically, this desire operates in the opposite direction, at least at first, and we know that scientific or technical (or artistic) discoveries or inventions are rarely motivated by a demand for security and equilibrium.

That demand wants rest, security and identity; the desire has no use for them, no success satisfies or stops it.

In order to reduce this objection, Bergson introduces the notion of an *élan vital*, a creative invention. This is where he leaves pragmatism behind, and exchanges a metaphysics of well-being for a teleology of life. This teleology is not new, it is romantic or pre-romantic, and has given up its all in the speculative dialectic.

But in the current state of science and techniques, resort to the entity 'Life' to cover what I call, for want of a better term, desire [*conatus, appetitio* for others], i.e. the complexification which disavows – de-authorizes, so to speak – all objects of demand in turn: resort to this term seems still far too derivative of human experience, too anthropomorphic. To say that a Life is responsible for the formation of systems such as the atom or the star or the cell or the human cortex or finally the collective cortex constituted by machine memories is contrary, as are all teleologies, to the materialist spirit, in the noble sense, Diderot's sense, which is the spirit of knowledge. It can only invoke chance and necessity, like Democritus and Lucretius. Matter does not go in for dialectic.

Obviously I do not intend to solve the problem. But if I invoke Democritus and Lucretius, this is because it seems to me that micro-physics and cosmology inspire in today's philosopher more a materialism than any teleology.

An immaterialist materialism, if it is true that matter is energy and mind is contained vibration.

One of the implications of this current of thinking is that it ought to deal another blow to what I shall call human narcissism. Freud already listed three famous ones: man is not the centre of the cosmos (Copernicus), is not the first living creature (Darwin), is not the master of meaning (Freud himself). Through contemporary techno-science, s/he learns that s/he does not have the monopoly of mind, that is of complexification, but that complexification is not inscribed as a destiny in matter, but as possible, and that it takes place, at random, but intelligibly, well before him/herself. S/he learns in particular that his/her own science is in its turn a complexification of matter, in which, so to speak, energy itself comes to be reflected, without humans necessarily getting any benefit from this. And that thus s/he must not consider him/herself as an origin or as a result, but as a transformer ensuring, through techno-science, arts, economic development, cultures and the new memorization they involve, a supplement of complexity in the universe.

This view can cause joy or despair. I should have liked to have had the time to show, through *Le rêve de d'Alembert*, for example, but many other texts too, that it was in its essentials the view of Diderot. It was also that of Marcel Duchamp and Stéphane Mallarmé. Perhaps it is enough, in all sobriety, to give us a reason for thinking and writing, and a love of matter. Matter in our effort performs its anamnesis.

4

Logos and *Techne*, or Telegraphy

The title *logos and techne* is as presumptuous as can be.

In the rubric for this conference, the organizers stress the impact of the so-called new technologies on the syntheses that constitute space and time. And in a preparatory note for the conference, Bernard Stiegler underlined three points:

1 technology is not, and probably never has been, a means for an end that would be science;
2 on the contrary (Habermas's) 'techno-science' is the present completion of a *tekhnologos* constitutively at work in the western *logos* (even if the Greek *tekhnai* were above all, at first, ways with language, logotechniques);
3 and finally, as the new technologies are now invading public space and common time (invading them in the form of industrial objects of production and consumption, including 'cultural' production and consumption), on a planetary scale, it is what we might call the most 'intimate' space-time, in its most 'elementary' syntheses, which is attacked, hounded and no doubt modified by the present state of technology.

I shall start from the basic hypothesis of Stiegler's work, namely that all technology is an 'objectification' – i.e. a spatialization – of meaning, whose model is writing itself, in the common sense of the word. And that inscription, putting into traces, on the one hand – because it is 'legible'

47

(decodable, if you like) – opens a public space of meaning and generates a community of users-producers, and on the other (?) because it is endowed with persistence by its being marked on a spatial support, conserves the sign of the past event, or rather produces it as available, presentable and reactualizable memory.

Starting from this point, what I want to do is to dissociate – with some formalism – several aspects of this memory-effect thus engendered by technique as inscription, referring it more particularly to the present state of techno-logos. I shall be doing this in a terminology that could be called materialist, and therefore metaphysical. I tell myself that this is for convenience, so as not to make the paper too severe. Possibly too the severity of the subject makes me incapable of doing any better.

I distinguish, then, without claiming that this is exhaustive, three sorts of memory-effects of technological inscription in general: breaching [*frayage*], scanning and passing, which coincide more or less with three very different sorts of temporal synthesis linked to inscription: habit, remembering [*rémémoration*] and anamnesis.

(1) Habit is an energetic set-up which is sometimes complex, of variable plasticity, which structures a certain type of behaviour in a certain type of contextual situation. The stability of the set-up allows the type of behaviour to be repeated with a significant saving of energy.

Psychologists and physiologists say that habit is acquired, contrary to other stable set-ups, such as instinct. But as you know, the distinction between these two sorts of set-up is not clear. For example, putting certain instincts to work can demand an apprenticeship or can at least be facilitated by it.

That is not my question, however. Habit rests on a breaching (whether or not genetically controlled), as they used to say a century ago, i.e. a putting into series of elements, for example neurons, nerve-zones and conductors in the case of vertebrate animals. Seen from a distance, this putting into series looks like a particular case of what ancient and classical astronomy and cosmology called attraction. Elements (stars, particles, cells, the individuals of a living species) which can be considered in isolation form a set which is notable for its double internal transcendence: the properties of the whole exceed those of the sum of the parts, and each element taken for itself is not exhausted by its definition as a part of a given totality. Attraction in the classical sense is itself a particular case of what general physical theory today calls interaction (in the nucleus, the atom, the molecule, the cell, the planetary system, the nebula, the galaxy, the cosmos). In classical philosophy this was also called reciprocal action.

You know how information and communication theory (cybernetics) since Neumann and Wiener allows a refinement of this concept of interaction, for example in the genetic regulation of the living organism, and what its impact has been on current conception and practice of social groups.

'Cultures', in the culturalist sense, can be considered as nebulae of habits whose continuing action on the individuals who are their elements is looked after by these stable energetic set-ups that contemporary anthropology calls structures. The structural laws which command the circulation (breaching) of words, goods and woman (following Levi-Stauss's trio) in a singular (idiomatic) way, when other ways are possible in principle, are norms of breaching. In traditional cultures, the habits thus commanded also include geographical and chronological elements – though it would be better to call them places and moments, named places and named moments, since by their construction these cultures are nebulae of habits inserted into a customary space-time. Customary like the native soil.

One of the questions posed insistently by Stiegler's note and the conference rubric, but also by an essay of Jean Chesneaux's, is that of the 'delocalization' and 'detemporalization' of breachings in the wake of the new technologies. This unanchoring began with the first 'technological revolution' which allowed industry (coal, steam and/or electricity) to spread across all cultures (more or less quickly, to greater or lesser depth) objects demanding modes (habits) of production, exchange and consumption which are possible and valid outside a given territory and a given moment.

Contemporary machines can accomplish operations which used to be called mental operations: taking in of data in terms

49

of information, and storing it (memorization), regulation of access to the information (what was known as 'recall'), calculations of possible effects according to different programmes, taking account of variables and choices (strategy). Any piece of data becomes useful (exploitable, operational) once it can be translated into information. This is just as much the case for so-called sensory data – colours and sounds – to the exact extent that their constitutive physical properties have been identified. After they have been put into digital form, these items of data can be synthesized anywhere and anytime to produce identical chromatic or acoustic products (simulacra). They are thereby rendered independent of the place and time of their 'initial' reception, realizable at a spatial and temporal distance: let's say telegraphable. The whole idea of an 'initial' reception, of what since Kant has been called an 'aesthetic', an empirical or transcendental mode whereby the mind is affected by a 'matter' which it does not fully control, which happens to it here and now – this whole idea seems completely out of date.

I shall not here follow this path of a profound crisis of aesthetics and therefore of the contemporary arts. As for memory-as-breaching, it is enough to point out two noteworthy facts:

(a) Current technology, that specific mode of tele-graphy, writing at a distance, removes the close contexts of which rooted cultures are woven. It is thus, through its specific manner of inscription, indeed productive of a sort of memorization freed from the supposedly immediate conditions of time and space. The question to follow here would be as follows: what is a body (body proper, social body) in tele-graphic culture? It calls up a spontaneous production of the past in habit, a tradition or transmission of ways of thinking, willing and feeling, a sort of breaching, then, which complicates, counters, neutralizes and extenuates earlier community breachings, and in any case translates them so as to move them on too, make them transmissible. If the earlier breachings remain there at all, resist a bit, they become subcultures. The question of a hegemonic teleculture on a world scale is already posed.

50

(b) The breachings corresponding to this culture have still to a large extent to be carried out for most human beings. This is why this culture raises questions. Stiegler is right to insist on the need to make its specific modes of inscription (and therefore of memorization) available to individuals. School used to teach future citizens how to write. What institution has responsibility for teaching tele-graphy? Can the ideal pursued by such an institution still be the citizen? Is an institution for the telegraphization of humans even possible? Is the idea of an institution not linked to the State and to reading and writing? And thus to the ideal of a political body? It is abundantly clear in any case that States are not the agencies in control of the general process of the new telegraphic breaching, which in principle goes well beyond them. Here we'd have to take up again the analysis – I'd say the metaphysical and ontological analysis – of capitalism. But these questions of apprenticeship and its control already some under a different memory-effect: not breaching but scanning.

(2) What I'm calling scanning here corresponds to the temporal synthesis that in classical philosophy and psychology was called remembering. As opposed to habit-breaching, the synthesis of remembering implies not only the retention of the past in the present as present, but the synthesis of the past as such and its reactualization as past in the present (of consciousness). Remembering implies the identification of what is remembered, and its classification in a calendar and a cartography.

In Kant's terms, there are not only the syntheses of apprehension and reproduction, but the synthesis of recognition. In Bergson's terms, there is not only the delay in the reaction to stimulus, not only the suspension and reserving of this reaction as potential (i.e. habit), but the grasp of this inhibited reaction even when it is not called up by the present situation. Which implies, in both descriptions, the intervention of a meta-agency which inscribes on itself, conserves and makes available the action–reaction pair independently of the present place and time. So this is already a tele-graphy – the concept in Kant, consciousness-cortex in Bergson. Today we

51

say that it is language in the strict sense, human language characterized by its double articulation, phonetic and semantic. On this approach, language is itself immediately grasped as technique, and a technique of a higher rank, a metatechnique. As opposed to simple breaching, language-memory implies properties unknown to habit: the denotation of what it retains (thanks to its symbolic transcription), recursivity (the combinations of signs are innumerable, starting from simple generative rules, its 'grammar'), and self-reference (language-signs can be denoted by language-signs: metalanguage). I believe that generative and transformational linguistics has got much closer to the technicity of language than has functionalist linguistics. For *techne* is the abstract from *tikto* which means *to engender, to generate* [*tekontes*, the genitors; *teknon*, the offspring].

It is perfectly possible to say that the living cell, and the organism with its organs, are already *tekhnai*, that 'life', as they say, is already technique: the fact remains that its 'language' (genetic code, say) not only limits the performance of this technique but also (in fact it's the same thing) does not allow it to be objectified, known and complexified in a controlled way. The history of life on earth cannot be assimilated to the history of technique in the common sense, because it has not proceeded by remembering but by breaching.

By virtue of the properties just listed, as indefinite *auto-techne*, language, because of the infinite capacity this implies for it, simultaneously reveals what is finite in every inscription, including its own. For every inscription demands the selection of what is inscribed. Linguistic structures themselves are operators of exclusion at all levels: phonematic, semantic, mythic, narrative, etc. With the *logike techne*, the *rhetorike techne* and the *poetike techne*, the Greeks, Aristotle, do not only determine the groups of rules to be observed in the arts of argumentation, persuasion and charm, they also unveil the finitude of these usages, and thereby uncover the infinite horizon of what is *to be said*, the infinite task of generating new sentences and rules. A task that was in those days called philosophy – funny word. Philosophy was then the agency of recognition, the meta- or tele-graphic agency that I have said is proper to 'active' memory, but that agency which appears as a quasi-institution in public space, which denotatively takes up and questions the culture of habit from which it emerges.

Technologos is therefore remembering, and not only habit. Its self-referential capacity, reflection in the usual sense, 'critical' reflection if you like, is exercised by remembering its own presuppositions and implications as its limitations. And by the same token, the *technologos* opens up the world of what has been excluded by its very constitution, by the structures of its functioning, at all levels. This is how new denotative linguistic genres are invented: arithmetic, geometry, analysis. This is how science is generated, the sciences, as a process of conquest of the unknown, of experimentation beyond traditional cultural experience, of complexification of the logos beyond the received *technologos* of breaching. This is the process I am calling scanning.

It is this, in its denotative form, which ends up by appearing as an institution in what we call research and development. Contemporary techno-science is the direct emanation of it, after centuries of hesitant formation. But now we know that it has 'taken', irreversibly.

The fact that this remembering is active, more and more active, exponentially active, is what philosophers know of modernity when they see in it the symptom of a hypertrophy of the will. The aspect of reactivity, so evident in breaching, fades in scanning. God, nature, destiny too are 'scanned'. And with them, the principle of a finality of the process of research and development. Any analogy of this process with that of a biological adaptation fails to stand up to reflection, because the latter is based on breaching alone. It is clear that with techno-science in its current state, it is a power to 'put in series' that is at work on planet Earth, and that the human race is its vehicle much more than its beneficiary. The human race even has to 'dehumanize' itself, in the sense that it is still a bio-cultural species, so as to rise to the new complexity, so as to become tele-graphic. The ethical problems raised by techno-science are there to prove that the question has already been raised. When you *can* simulate *in vitro* the explosion of the sun or the fertilization or gestation of a living

53

creature, you have to decide what you *want*. And we just *don't know*. This foreclosure of ends is there in the principle of scanning. It has been dressed up in all sorts of disguises: destination of man, progress, enlightenment, emancipation, happiness. Today this foreclosure appears naked. More knowledge and power, yes – but why, no.

Can a *telekoinonia*, a telegraphic community without telos, be constituted around or out of this foreclosure?

(3) Finally, a few words about 'passing'. This is another memorization, linked to a writing which is different from the inscription by breaching or experimentation, different from habitual repetition or voluntary remembering. I use the term 'passing' with an allusion to the third memorizing technique that Freud opposes to the first two in his text on 'psychoanalytical technique': the (infinitive) 'passing' here is the German *durch*, as in *Durcharbeitury*, or the *through* of the English *working through*, the passing through of *trans*- or *per*-laboration.

This word 'work', widely used since Freud, is very deceptive. There is also work in every technique: there is no breaching or scanning without some expenditure of energy. If it is true that passing certainly uses up more force than other techniques, this is because it is a technique with no rule, or a negative rule, deregulation. A generativity with, if possible, no set-up other than the absence of set-up.

The logos itself, in that technology, will have to be turned not on itself, as in scanning, to purposes of appropriation and expansion, but turned against itself to the extent that it is 'bound', as Freud said, synthesized at all levels, from the phonematic to the argumentative and the rhetorical. The point is precisely to pass beyond synthesis in general.

Or, if you like, to pass beyond the reminder of what has been forgotten. The point would be to recall what could not have been forgotten because it was not inscribed. Is it possible to recall if it was not inscribed? Does it even make sense? And is it a technological task, a task for the *technologos*?

In any case, you will agree that this is a pretty good tele-graphy, an inscription from afar, from very far, and for very far, in time and space. And we know this 'afar' is not light years away, it can and must be very close, in the very question left hanging by experimental scanning, and the secret of the foreclosure that underlies it.

You see what I'm talking about here: what psychoanalysis calls anamnesis, what so-called 'French thought' has been calling *writing* for a long time. I do not take this 'passing' to be a transgression, and this is why I took my distance (perhaps too quickly) from Bataille and Klossowski. This is how I'd like to formulate it in this 'materialist' approach to technologies I'm taking today.

It makes sense to try to recall something (let's call it something) which has not been inscribed if the inscription of this something *broke* the support of the writing or the memory. I'm borrowing this metaphor of the mirror from one of the treatises of Dôgen's *Shobôgenzô*, the *Zenki*: there can be a presence that the mirror cannot reflect, but that breaks it to smithereens. A foreigner or a Chinese can come before the mirror and their image appear in it. But if what Dôgen calls 'a clear mirror' faces the mirror, then 'everything will break into smithereens.' And Dôgen goes on to make this clearer: 'Do not imagine that is first the time in which the breaking has not yet happened, nor that there is then the time in which everything breaks. There is just the breaking.' So there is a breaking presence which is never inscribed nor memorable. It does not appear. It is not a forgotten inscription, it does not have its place and time on the support of inscriptions, in the reflecting mirror. It remains unknown to breachings and scannings.

I am not sure that the West – the philosophical West – has succeeded in thinking this, by the very fact of its technological vocation. Plato, perhaps, when he tries to think *agathon* beyond essence. Freud perhaps when he tries to think primary repression. But both always threatening to fall back into the *technologos*. Because they try to find 'the word that gets rid', as Dôgen writes. And even the late Heidegger is perhaps missing the violence of the breaking; it is perhaps too comfortable to call the effect of the clear mirror of Being on the mirror of beings a 'clearing'.

I am not sure that the exhausting work of Oedipus towards the presence that broke his memory, the god's word, deserves the name of perlaboration or anamnesis. It all depends on the way the word of Apollo is 'situated' in the development of Oedipus's life. This is the whole question of Freud's *Nachträglichkeit*: was the first blow – which, as you know, was not recorded and only comes back as second blow, disguised – struck on the same surface on which the second and following blows will be inscribed, differing from them only in that it is undecipherable? These terms 'first' and 'second' are terrible, because they put the clear mirror and the mirror on an equal footing.

Anamnesis would be this notification, this warning, or obligation [*mnaomai, mnômai*; in Latin *monere, monimentum*] to stand up [*ana-*] towards the clear mirror, through the breaking.

It is possible to have serious reservations about Freud's conception of anamnesis, and I confess I have such reservations in one sense. The fact remains that, as though by chance, the writings on psychoanalytical technique which have provided me, as you'll have recognized, with the trilogy that has been guiding me – repetition, remembering, working through – these *technical* writings teach what technology must be when the aim is to make passing or anamnesis possible. For the psychoanalyst, it is listening with a third ear, removing all the pre-inscriptions of the other two (stopping them up), abandoning the already established syntheses, at whatever level: logical, rhetorical and even linguistic, and letting work in a free-floating way what passes: the signifier, however senseless it may appear.

They only thing I can see that can bear comparison with this a-technical or a-technological rule is writing, itself an anamnesis of what has not been inscribed. For it offers to inscription the white of the paper, blank like the neutrality of the analytical ear.

Except that it tries to blank out too the so-called free associations themselves.

I will not here develop this extraordinarily intricate and intriguing problem. We envisage this writing as passing or anamnesis in both writers and artists (it's clearly Cézanne's working-through) as a resistance (in what I think is a non-psychoanalytical sense, more like that of Wilson in

Orwell's *1984*) to the syntheses of breaching and scanning. A resistance to clever programmes and fat telegrams. The whole question is this: is the passage possible, will it be possible with, or allowed by, the new mode of inscription and memoration that characterizes the new technologies? Do they not impose syntheses, and syntheses conceived still more intimately in the soul than any earlier technology has done? But by that very fact, do they not also help to refine our anamnesic resistance? I'll stop on this vague hope, which is too dialectical to take seriously. All this remains to be thought out, tried out.

5

Time Today

I

The title *Time Today* is not without paradox. *Today* is a time designator, a deictic indexing time in the same way as 'now', 'yesterday', etc. Like all temporal deictics, it operates by referring what it designates to the sole present of the sentence itself, or to the sentence only in so far as it is present. It temporalizes the referent of the present sentence by situating it exclusively with respect to the time in which this sentence is taking place, which is the present. And without at all having recourse to the time *in which* the sentence could in its turn be located, for example by means of a clock or a calendar. In this latter case, sentence 1 could itself be taken as referent of another sentence 2, which would say, for example, 'Sentence 1 took place on the 24 June.' Calendar and clock constitute networks of 'objective' time which allow the moment of sentence 2 to be located without reference to the time 'of' sentence 1. Even supposing that a new sentence (3) makes no use of dates and hours to refer to sentence 1 (for example (sentence 3): 'sentence 1 was uttered yesterday', in which the event of sentence 1 is indeed located by reference to the present of sentence 3 alone), the fact remains that sentence 1 is put in the position of being designated by the deictic 'yesterday'. Sentence 1 is no longer the presenting present, it becomes that present 'then presenting and now presented', in other words the past.

As an occurrence, each sentence is a 'now'. It presents, now, a meaning, a referent, a sender and an addressee. With respect to presentation, we must imagine the time of an occurrence as – and only as – present. This present cannot be grasped as such, it is absolute. It cannot be synthesized *directly* with other presents. The other presents with which it can be placed in relation are necessarily and immediately changed into presented presents, i.e. past.

When the time of presentation is glossed and we reach the conclusion that 'each' sentence appears at each time, we omit the inevitable transformation of present into past, and we place all the moments together on a single diachronic line.

We thus let ourselves slip from the presenting time implied in 'each' occurrence, to the presented time it has become or, better, from time as 'now' [*nun*] to time considered as 'this time' [*dieses Mal*], an expression which presupposes that 'one time' [*einmal*] is equivalent to 'that time' [*das andere Mal*]. What is forgotten in this objectifying synthesis is that *it* takes place *now*, in the presenting occurrence that effects the synthesis, and that this 'now' is not *yet* one of the 'times' it presents along the diachronic line.

Because it is absolute, the presenting present cannot be grasped: it is *not yet* or *no longer* present. It is always too soon or too late to grasp presentation itself and present it. Such is the specific and paradoxical constitution of the event. That something happens, the occurrence, means that the mind is disappropriated. The expression 'it happens that . . .' is the formula of non-mastery of self over self. The event makes the self incapable of taking possession and control of what it is. It testifies that the self is essentially passible to a recurrent alterity.

With its title *Time Today*, my discourse is clearly placed under the aegis of this passibility. It has not at all the object of exercising a complete control over the referent it designates, time – not even in theory. My intention is only that of trying to bring out some of the ways in which modernity deals with the temporal condition.

II

This brief reminder of the question of time, from the point of view of presentation, is conceptually marked by the privilege it accords to discontinuity, to 'discreteness' and to difference. It is clear that this description presupposes, as its opposite and complement, the ability to gather and retain, at least potentially, in a single 'presence', a certain number of distinct moments. As the word suggests, consciousness implies memory, in the Husserlian sense of an elementary *Retention*. By opposing discontinuity with synthesis, consciousness seems to be the very thing that throws down a challenge to alterity. In this conflict, what is at stake is to determine the limits within which consciousness is capable of embracing a diversity of moments (of 'information', as we say these days) and of actualizing them 'each time' they are needed.

There is good reason to assume two extreme limits to the capacity to synthesize a multiplicity of information, the one minimal, the other maximal. Such is the major intuition which guides Leibniz's work, and in particular the *Monadology*. God is the absolute monad to the extent that he conserves in complete retention the totality of information constituting the world. And if divine retention is to be complete, it must also include those pieces of information not yet presented to the incomplete monads, such as our minds, and which remain to come in what we call the future. In this perspective, the 'not yet' is due only to the limit on the faculty of synthesis available to the intermediary monads. For the absolute memory of God, the future is always already given. We can thus conceive, for the temporal condition, an upper limit determined by a perfect recording or archival capacity. As consummate archivist, God is outside time, and this is one of the grounds of modern Western metaphysics.

Modern Western physics, for its part, finds its ground on the side of the other limit. One can imagine a being incapable of recording and using past information by inserting it between the event and its effect: a being, then, which could only convey or transmit the 'bits' of information as they are received. In these conditions, in the absence of any interfacing filter between input and output, such a being would be situated at the degree zero of consciousness or memory. This is the being Leibniz calls a 'material point'. It represents the simplest unit required by the science of movement, mechanics. In contemporary physics and astrophysics, the family of elementary particles is constituted of entities about as 'naked' (the word is Leibniz's) as the material point.

The fact remains that each subset of particles included in this family presents properties allowing the elements to enter into relation with others according to specific regularities. This specificity means that a particle has a sort of elementary memory and consequently a temporal filter. This is why contemporary physicists tend to think that time emanates from matter itself, and that it is not an entity outside or inside the universe whose function it would be to gather all different times into universal history. It is only in certain regions that such – partial – syntheses could be detected. There would on this view be areas of determinism where complexity is growing.

On this approach, the human brain and language are the sign that humanity is a complex of this sort, temporary and highly improbable. And it then becomes tempting to think that what is called research and development in contemporary society and the results of which constantly disturb our environment are much more the result of such a process of 'cosmolocal' complexification than the work of human genius attached to the discovery of truth and the realization of good.

III

I should like to develop a little that aspect of the hypothesis which is most particularly relative to our theme, 'time today'. It seems to me that the anxiety prevalent today in the philosophical and political domain about 'communication', *kommunikative Handeln*, 'pragmatics', transparency in the expression of opinions, etc., has practically no relation with the 'classical' philosophical and politocological problems relative to the foundation of *Gemeinschaft* [community], *Mitsein* [being together], and even of *Öffentlichkeit* [public space] as thought by the Enlightenment.

61

If we are to interrogate properly this compulsion to communicate and to secure the communicability of anything at all (objects, services, values, ideas, languages, tastes) which is expressed in particular in the context of the new technologies, we must, I think, give up the philosophy of the emancipation of humanity implied by 'classical' modern metaphysics. All technology, beginning with writing considered as a *techne*, is an artefact allowing its users to stock more information, to improve their competence and optimize their performances.

The importance of the technologies constructed around electronics and data processing resides in the fact that they make the programming and control of memorizing, i.e. the synthesis of different times in one time, less dependent on the conditions of life on earth. It is very probable that among the material complexes we know, the human brain is the most capable of producing complexity in its turn, as the production of the new technologies proves. And as such, it also remains the supreme agency for controlling these technologies.

And yet its own survival requires that it be fed by a body, which in turn can survive only in the conditions of life on earth, or in a simulacrum of those conditions. I think that one of the essential objectives of research today is to overcome the obstacle that the body places in the way of the development of communicational technologies, i.e. the new extended memory. In particular, this could be the real stake of research bearing on fertility, gestation, birth, illness, death, sex, sport, etc. All seem to converge on the same aim, that of making the body adaptable to non-terrestrial conditions of life, or of substituting another 'body' for it.

Having said this, if we consider the considerable change to which our culture is subjected today, we will observe to what extent, analogically, the new technologies are unblocking the obstacle constituted by human life on earth. Ethnocultures were for a long time the apparatuses for memorizing information such that peoples were able to organize their space and their time. They were, notably, the way in whichmultiplicities of different times could be gathered and conserved in a single memory (Bernard Stiegler). Themselves considered as *technai*, they allowed collections of individuals

62

and generations to have real stocks of information at their disposal through time and space. In particular they produced the specific organization of temporality that we call historical narratives. There are many ways of telling a story, but the narrative as such can be considered to be a technical apparatus giving a people the means to store, order and retrieve units of information, i.e. events. More precisely, narratives are like temporal filters whose function is to transform the emotive charge linked to the event into sequences of units of information capable of giving rise to something like meaning. I shall return to this.

Now it is clear that these cultural apparatuses which constitute relatively extensive forms of memory remain tightly bound to the historical and geographical context in which they operate. This context furnishes that memory with most of the events which it must seize, stock, neutralize and make available. Traditional culture thus remains profoundly marked by its local situation on the surface of the earth so that it cannot easily be transplanted or communicated. As is well known, this inertia constitutes a major aspect of the problems linked today to the general phenomenon of immigration and emigration.

The new technologies, on the other hand, in as much as they furnish cultural models which are not initially rooted in the local context but are immediately formed in view of the broadest diffusion across the surface of the globe, provide a remarkable means of overcoming the obstacle traditional culture opposes to the recording, transfer and communication of information.

It scarcely seems that this generalized accessibility offered by the new cultural goods is strictly speaking a progress. The penetration of techno-scientific apparatus into the cultural field in no way signifies an increase of knowledge, sensibility, tolerance and liberty. Reinforcing this apparatus does not liberate the spirit, as the *Aufklärung* thought. Experience shows rather the reverse: a new barbarism, illiteracy and impoverishment of language, new poverty, merciless remodelling of opinion by the media, immiseration of the mind, obsolescence of the soul, as Walter Benjamin and Theodor Adorno repeatedly stressed.

63

Which is not to say that one can be content, with the Frankfurt School, to criticize the subordination of the mind to the rules and values of the culture-industry. Be it positive or negative, this diagnosis still belongs to a humanist point of view. The facts are ambiguous. 'Postmodern' culture is in fact on the way to spreading to all humanity. But to this same extent it is tending to abolish local and singular experience, it hammers the mind with gross stereotypes, apparently leaving no place for reflection and education.

If the new culture can produce such divergent effects, of generalization *and* destruction, this is because it seems to belong to the human domain neither by its aims nor its origins. As is clearly shown by the development of the techno-scientific system, technology and the culture associated with it are under a necessity to pursue their rise, and this necessity must be referred to the process of complexification (of neg-entropy) which takes place in the area of the cosmos inhabited by humanity. The human race is, so to speak, 'pulled forward' by this process without possessing the slightest capacity for mastering it. It has to adapt to the new conditions. It is even probable that this has always been the case throughout human history. And if we can become aware of that fact today, this is because of the exponential growth affecting sciences and technology.

The electronic and information network spread over the earth gives rise to a global capacity for memorizing which must be estimated at the cosmic scale, without common measure with that of traditional cultures. The paradox implied by this memory resides in the fact that in the last analysis it is nobody's memory. But 'nobody' here means that the body supporting that memory is no longer an earth-bound body. Computers never stop being able to synthesize more and more 'times', so that Leibniz could have said of this process that it is on the way to producing a monad much more 'complete' than humanity itself has ever able to be.

The human race is already in the grip of the necessity of having to evacuate the solar system in 4.5 billion years. It will have been the transitory vehicle for an extremely improbable process of complexification. The exodus is already on the agenda. The only chance of success lies in the species' adapting itself to the complexity that challenges it. And if the exodus succeeds, what it will have preserved is not the species itself but the 'most complete monad' with which it was pregnant.

IV

You will smile at how much the picture I have drawn owes to fiction. I should like to sketch out a few 'realistic' implications it has by returning to the opening question: how is time synthesized in our thought and practice today?

I return to the 'Leibnizian' hypothesis. The more complete a monad, the more numerous the data it memorizes, thus becoming capable of mediating what happens before reacting, and thus becoming less directly dependent on the event. So the more complete the monad, the more the incoming event is neutralized. For a monad supposed to be perfect, like God, there are in the end no bits of information at all. God has nothing to learn. In the mind of God, the universe is instantaneous.

The growth of techno-scientific systems appears to be drawn by this ideal of *Mathesis Universalis* or, to use Borges's metaphor, the library of Babel. Complete information means neutralizing more events. What is already known cannot, in principle, be experienced as an event. Consequently, if one wants to control a process, the best way of so doing is to subordinate the present to what is (still) called the 'future', since in these conditions the 'future' will be completely predetermined and the present itself will cease opening onto an uncertain and contingent 'afterwards'.

Better: what comes 'after' the 'now' will have to come 'before' it. In as much as a monad in thus saturating its memory is stocking the future, the present loses its privilege of being an ungraspable point from which, however, time should always distribute itself between the 'not yet' of the future and the 'no longer' of the past.

Now there is a model of such a temporal situation. It is offered by the daily practice of exchange. Someone (X) gives someone (Y) an object a at time t. This giving has as its condition that Y will give X an object *b* at time *t'*. I leave to one side here the classical question of knowing how *a* and *b* can be made equivalent. What is not irrelevant for us here is the fact that the first phase of the exchange takes place if and only if the second is perfectly guaranteed, to the point that it can be considered to have already happened.

There are many 'language games' – I prefer to say 'genres of discourse' – in which a later defined occurrence is expected, promised, etc., at the time the first takes place. But in the case of exchange, the 'second' occurrence, the payment, is not expected at the time of the first, it is presupposed as the condition of the 'first'. In this manner, the future conditions the present. Exchange requires that what is future be as if it were present. Guarantees, insurance policies, security are means of neutralizing the case as occasional, or, as we say, to forestall eventualities [*prévenir l'ad-venir*]. According to this way of treating time, suc-cess depends on the informational pro-cess, which consists in making sure that, at time *t'*, nothing can happen other than the occurrence programmed at time *t*.

As for the lapse of time between *t'* and *t*, we can say that it is irrelevant to the essential principle of exchange we have just recalled. But it is none the less interesting, it must be said, in that it commands interest. The more the temporal gap increases, the more the chance increases of something unexpected happening – the greater the risk. The growth of risk can itself be calculated in terms of probability and in turn translated into monetary terms. Money here appears as what it really is, time stocked in view of forestalling what comes about. I shall not develop this idea further here.

Let us say merely that what is called capital is grounded in the principle that money is nothing other than time placed in reserve, available. It matters little whether this be after the event or in advance of what is called 'real time'. 'Real time' is only the moment at which the time conserved in the form of money is realized. What is important for capital is not the time already invested in goods and services, but the time still stored in stocks of 'free' or 'fresh' money, given that this represents the only time which can be used with a view to organizing the future and neutralizing the event.

We can say, then, that there is a tight and relevant correlation of what I have called the monad in expansion, produced by the techno-scientific apparatus, with the predominance of capitalism in the most 'developed' societies and, in particular, with the use of money in them. Capital must be seen not only as a major figure of human history, but also as the effect, observable on the earth, of a cosmic process of complexification. What is at stake with capitalism is certainly to make exchange and communication between human beings more flexible, as can be seen with the abandoning of the gold-standard in the evaluation of currency and the adoption of electronic methods of accountancy, by the institution of multinationals, etc. So many signs of the necessity of complexifying relations between human beings. Where can this come from if it is true that these results are not always profitable to humanity in general, nor even to the fraction of humanity supposed to benefit directly from them? Why do we have to save money and time to the point where this imperative seems like the law of our lives? Because saving (at the level of the system as a whole) allows the system to increase the quantity of money given over to anticipating the future. This is particularly the case with the capital invested in research and development. The enjoyment of humanity must, it is clear, be sacrificed to the interests of the monad in expansion.

Among the many effects of this undeniable hegemony, I shall mention only one. From its origins, mankind has set up a specific means of controlling time – the narrative of myth. Myth allows a sequence of events to be placed in a constant framework in which the beginning and the end of a story form a sort of rhythm or rhyme, as Hölderlin put it. The idea of destiny long prevalent in human communities – and even today in the unconscious, if we are to believe Freud – presupposes the existence of a timeless agency which 'knows' in its totality the succession of moments constituting a life, be it individual or collective. What will happen is predetermined in the divine oracle, and human beings have as their only task that of unfolding identities already constituted in synchrony or achrony. Although given out at the time of Oedipus's birth, Apollo's oracle none the less prescribes in advance the destiny

67

of the hero up until his death. This initial and summary attempt to neutralize the unexpected occurrence was abandoned as the techno-scientific spirit and the figure of capitalism came to maturity, both of them much more efficient in controlling time.

Very different, and yet very close, is the way modernity treats the problem. Modernity is not, I think, a historical period, but a way of shaping a sequence of moments in such a way that it accepts a high rate of contingency. It is not without significance that this formulation can be verified in works as diverse as those of Augustine, Kant and Husserl. The description of the temporal synthesis that I sketched out to begin with also belongs to modernity thus understood.

But what merits attention is that modern metaphysics none the less gave birth to the reconstitution of great narratives – Christianity, Enlightenment, romanticism, German speculative idealism, Marxism – which are not entirely foreign to mythical narratives. They do, certainly, imply that the future remains open as the ultimate aim of human history, under the name of emancipation. But they retain from myth the principle according to which the general course of history is conceivable.

The modern narrative, to be sure, induces a more political than ritual attitude. The fact remains that the ideal situated at the end of the narrative of emancipation is supposedly conceivable, even if it comprises, under the name of freedom, a sort of void or 'blank', a lack of definition, to be safeguarded. In other terms, destination [*Bestimmung*] is not destiny. But both designate a diachronic series of events whose 'reason' at least is judged to be explicable, on the one hand as destiny, by tradition, on the other as task, by political philosophy.

Unlike myth, the modern project certainly does not ground its legitimacy in the past, but in the future. And it is thus that it offers a better hold for the process of complexification. Having said this, it is one thing to project human emancipation, and another to programme the future as such. Liberty is not security. What some people have called the postmodern perhaps merely designates a break, or at least a splitting, between one pro- and the other – between project and programme. The latter seems today much better able than the former to meet the challenge thrown down to humanity by the process of complexification. But among the events which the programme attempts to neutralize as much as it can one must, alas, also count the unforeseeable effects engendered by the contingency and freedom proper to the human project.

V

As is only fitting, I shall not have the time to 'conclude' the argument. Let it suffice to say how foreign to my own way of thinking is the Leibnizian hypothesis I have just presented. A few 'theses' will show this briefly in conclusion.

(1) The techno-scientific apparatus which Heidegger calls the *Gestell* does indeed 'accomplish' metaphysics, as he writes. The principle of reason, the *Satz vom Grund*, locates reason in the field of 'physics' by virtue of the – metaphysical – postulate that every event in the world is to be explained as the effect of a cause and that reason consists in determining that cause (or that 'reason'), i.e. rationalizing the given and neutralizing the future. What are called the human sciences, for example, have become largely a branch of physics. Mind and even soul are studied as though they were interfaces in physical processes, and this is how computers are starting to be able to deliver simulacra of certain mental operations.

(2) Capital is not an economic and social phenomenon. It is the shadow cast by the principle of reason on human relations. Prescriptions such as: communicate, save time and money, control and forestall the event, increase exchanges, are all likely to extend and reinforce the 'great monad'. That 'cognitive' discourse has conquered hegemony over other genres, that in ordinary language, the pragmatic and inter-relational aspect comes to the fore, whilst 'the poetic' appears to deserve less and less attention – all these features of the contemporary language-condition cannot be understood as effects of a simple modality of exchange, i.e. the one called 'capitalism' by economic and historical science. They are the

signs that a new use of language is taking place, the stake of which is that of knowing objects as precisely as possible and of realizing among ordinary speakers a consensus as broad as that supposed to reign in the scientific community.

As for knowledge, any object will do, but on a double condition: first that one can refer to this object in a logically and mathematically consistent vocabulary and syntax, the rules and terms of which can be communicated with minimal ambiguity; and, next, that some proof can be administered of the reality of the objects referred to by the propositions thus formed, by exhibiting sensory data judged relevant with respect to these objects.

The first condition has not only given birth to the remarkable rise of logical and mathematical formalism seen since the middle of the last century. It has also allowed the accreditation of new objects or new idealities (let's say new sentences) in mathematical and logical culture, and thus brought out new problems. The fact that it is now possible to formulate a good number of paradoxes that left the tradition in perplexity is the indubitable sign that the complexification of symbolic languages is progressing, and that the sciences are now appropriating objects which previously they ignored. It will be noted that many paradoxes belong more or less closely to the problematic of time. It suffices to mention questions such as that of recurrence (the use of the enigmatic expression 'and so on . . .'), in particular in the argumentation of the liar paradox (which Russell eliminates with his theory of types), the development of logics and linguistics of time which allow the difficult problems of modality to be solved or better posed, the mathematics of catastrophes (René Thom), the theory of relativity . . . .

As for the second condition required by 'cognitive' language, which is the necessity of administering the proof of the assertion, it carries the implication that the technologies be continually developed. For if the propositions to be verified (or falsified) are to be more and more sophisticated, then the apparatus given the task of providing relevant sensory data must be indefinitely refined and complexified. Particle physics, electronics and data processing are today indispensable for conceiving (and realizing) most 'machines for proving'. I observe that capitalism is powerfully interested in this question of the proof. For the technologies required by the scientific process open the way for the production and distribution of new commodities, either directly committed to scientific research, or modified with a view to popular use. To this extent at least, means of knowledge become means of production, and capital appears as the most powerful, if it is not the only, apparatus for realizing the complexity attained in the field of cognitive languages. Capital does not govern the knowledge of reality, but it gives reality to knowledge.

It is often thought that if the economic system is led to behave in this way, it is because it is guided by the thirst for profit. And indeed, the use of scientific technologies in industrial production allows an increase in the quantities of surplus-value by saving on labour-time. Yet it seems that the 'ultimate' motor of this movement is not essentially of the order of human desire: it consists rather in the process of negentropy which appears to 'work' the cosmic area inhabited by the human race. One could go so far as to say that the desire for profit and wealth is no doubt no other than this process itself, working upon the nervous centres of the human brain and experienced directly by the human body.

(3) Thought today appears to be required to take part in the process of rationalization. Any other manner of thinking is condemned, isolated and rejected as irrational. Since the Renaissance and the classical age, let's say Galileo and Descartes, a latent conflict has opposed rationality to other ways of thinking and writing, and notably to metaphysics and literature. With the Vienna Circle, war is openly declared. In the name of the same motif, that of 'overcoming metaphysics', Carnap on the one hand and Heidegger on the other cut Western philosophy in two, logical positivism and poetic 'ontologie'. This break essentially affects the nature of language. Is language an instrument destined *par excellence* to provide the mind with the most exact knowledge of reality and to control as far as possible its transformation? In that case the true task of philosophy consists in helping science to free itself from the inconsistencies of natural languages by constructing a pure and univocal symbolic language. Or ought

71

language to be thought after the fashion of a field of perception, capable of 'making sense' by itself independently of any intention to signify? Sentences, in that case, far from being under the responsibility of the speakers, should rather be thought of as discontinuous and spasmodic concretions of a continuous 'speaking medium', like Heidegger's *Sage*, that same medium called on by Malraux and Merleau-Ponty under the name of 'voices of silence', a medium that in French we would call *langagier* rather than *linguistique*.

We can say that the first option fits up to a point with the type of 'rationality' demanded by the monad in expansion. But what limits its perfect merging with complexity is the remains of humanist philosophy which is paradoxically written into the principle that language is an instrument used by the human mind. For it is possible, and has been the case, that a good number of propositions, even though well formed and well established according to the criteria of the new sciences, are at first sight neither useful nor obvious to the human mind. Now this very difficulty can precisely be seen as a sign that the real 'user' of language is not the human mind *qua* human, but complexity in movement, of which mind is only a transitory support. It does not follow from communicating in general and from making every assertion communicable that a greater transparency of the human community to itself is favoured; it follows simply that a greater number of pieces of information can be combined with others so that their totality comes to form an operational, flexible and efficient system – the monad.

As for the second option, which I called ontological, it is by its nature turned towards those modes of language which do not aim solely to describe exhaustively the objects to which they refer. Among these language modes, one can mention, for various reasons, free conversation, reflexive judgement and meditation, free association (in the psychoanalytical sense), the poetic and literature, music, the visual arts, everyday language. What matters in these modes is clearly the fact that all should generate occurrences before knowing the rules of this generativity, and that some of them even have no concern for determining those rules. This is the fact that Kant and the Romantics, especially, thematized under the rubric of genius, of a nature acting in the mind itself. One can also refer the discursive genres I'm talking about to the principle of a productive imagination. But it will be noted that such an imagination plays no less a role in science itself, the role of the heuristic moment it needs if it is to progress. What these diverse or even heterogeneous forms have in common is the freedom and the lack of preparation with which language shows itself capable of receiving what can happen in the 'speaking medium', and of being accessible to the event. To the point at which one can wonder whether the true complexity does not consist in this passibility rather than in the activity of 'reducing and constructing' language, as Carnap proposed to do.

Finally, a rationality does not deserve its name if it denies its part in the open passibility and uncontrolled creativity there is in most languages, including the cognitive. To the extent that it really does comprise such a denial, technical, scientific and economic rationality would deserve the name of 'ideology', if that term did not in turn carry too many metaphysical presuppositions. Anyway, it is certain that the model of consensus which, it is claimed, is borrowed from the argumentative community of the sciences and is proposed as an ideal for human sciences shows to what extent that 'rationality' exercises its hegemony over the diversity of discursive genres which language has in potential. This rationality can only be said to be rational if one has accepted as sole value the performativity which commands the logic of the great monad faced with the cosmological challenge.

(4) It will come as no surprise that the hypothesis I adopt is the second. Being prepared to receive what thought is not prepared to think is what deserves the name of thinking. As I have said, this attitude is to be found in reputedly rational language as much as in the poetic, in art, ordinary language, if, that is, it is essential to the cognitive discourse to progress.

One cannot, consequently, admit the crude separation of sciences and arts prescribed by modern Western culture. As we know, it has as its corollary the relegation of the arts and literature to the miserable function of distracting human beings from what hounds and harrasses them all the time, i.e.

the obsession of controlling time. I know that the resistance one can oppose to the process of formation and expansion of the great monad will do nothing to change this. But it must never be forgotten that if thinking indeed consists in receiving the event, it follows that no-one can claim to think without being *ipso facto* in a position of resistance to the procedures for controlling time.

To think is to question everything, including thought, and question, and the process. To question requires that something happen that reason has not yet known. In thinking, one accepts the occurrence for what it is: 'not yet' determined. One does not prejudge it, and there is no security. Peregrination in the desert. One cannot write without bearing witness to the abyss of time in its coming.

In this respect, we must distinguish two ways of assuming the questioning, according as the stress is or is not placed on the urgency of the reply. The principle of reason is the way of questioning which rushes to its goal, the reply. It involves a sort of impatience in the single presupposition that in any case one can always find a 'reason' or a cause for every question. Non-Western traditions of thought have a quite different attitude. What counts in their manner of questioning is not at all to determine the reply as soon as possible, to seize and exhibit some object which will count as the cause of the phenomenon in question. But to be and remain questioned by it, to stay through meditation responsive to it, without neutralizing by explanation its power of disquiet. In the very heart of Western culture, such an attitude has, or had, its analogue in the manner of being and thinking which issued from the Judaic tradition. What this tradition calls 'study' and 'reading' requires that any reality be treated as an obscure message addressed by an unknowable or even unnameable agency. As to a verse of the Torah, one must listen to the phenomenon, decipher and interpret it, of course, but with humour, without forgetting that this interpretation will itself be interpreted as a message no less enigmatic, Levinas would say no less marvellous, than the initial event. Derrida's problematic of deconstruction and *différance*, Deleuze's principle of nomadism belong, however different they may be, to this approach to time. In it, time remains uncontrolled, does not give rise to work, or at least not in the customary sense of the word 'work'.

A last remark on what has been called passibility. It would be presumptuous, not to say criminal, for a thinker or a writer to claim to be the witness or guarantor of the event. It must be understood that what testifies is not at all the entity, whatever it be, which claims to be in charge of this passibility to the event, but the event 'itself'. What memorizes or retains is not a capacity of the mind, not even accessibility to what occurs, but, in the event, the ungraspable and undeniable 'presence' of a something which is other than mind and which, 'from time to time', occurs . . . .

(5) Heidegger tried to ground the resistance I am talking about on the Greek model of art understood as *techne*. However, since Plato, art or *Dichtung* has been conceived of as a remodelling, a *plattein*, and it has been the principal mode in which politics has sought to fashion the community according to this or that metaphysical ideal. Following Lacoue-Labarthe in this, I think that there exists a narrow and essential correlation between the art of politics and the fine arts. An outstanding case of this combination is to be found in Plato's *Republic:* the problem of politics consists only in observing the correct model, which is the model of the Good, in fashioning the human community. *Mutatis mutandis*, the same principle is to be found in the political philosophies of the Middle Ages, the Renaissance and modernity.

Nazism in a sense reversed the relation: here it is 'art' which explicitly stands in for politics. As is well known, the Nazis made a widespread and systematic use of myth, of the media, of mass culture and the new technologies with a view to bringing about the total mobilization of energy in all its forms. In this way they inscribe in facts the Wagnerian dream of 'the total work of art'. Syberberg has shown that the *Gesamtkunstwerk* is realized in the cinema, in *tele-techne* in general, much more than in opera. Politics today, with different justifications, sometimes with opposite arguments, is of the same nature. In what is called modern democracy, there persists the hegemony of the principle according to

which the opinion of the masses must be seduced and led by
what I would call 'tele-graphic' procedures, by the various
types of 'inscription-at-a-distance' descriptions and prescriptions. And in this sense, one Nazism has won: as total
mobilization.

(6) In so far as they do not allow themselves to be subordinated to 'tele-graphy', thought and writing are isolated and
placed in the ghetto, in the sense in which the work of Kafka
deploys that theme. But this term 'ghetto' is not here simply
a metaphor. The Jews of Warsaw were not only doomed to
death, they also had to pay for the 'protection measures'
taken against them, starting with the wall that the Nazis
decided to erect against the supposed threat of a typhoid
epidemic. The same goes for writers and thinkers: if they
resist the predominant use of time today, they are not only
predestined to disappear, but they must also contribute to the
making of a 'sanitary cordon' isolating themselves. In the
shelter of this cordon, their destruction is supposed to be able
to be put off for a while. But they 'buy' this brief and vain
delay by modifying their way of thinking and writing in such
a way that their works become more or less communicable,
exchangeable; in a word, commercializable. But the exchange,
the buying and selling of ideas and words, does not fail to
contribute, contradictorily to the 'final solution' of the
problem: how to write, how to think? I mean that they
contribute to making even more hegemonic the great rule of
controlled time. It follows that public space, *Öffentlichkeit*, in
these conditions, stops being the space for experiencing,
testing and affirming the state of a mind open to the event,
and in which the mind seeks to elaborate an idea of that state
itself, especially under the sign of the 'new'. Public space
today is transformed into a market of cultural commodities,
in which 'the new' has become an additional source of
surplus-value.

(7) When the point is to extend the capacities of the monad,
it seems reasonable to abandon, or even actively to destroy,
those parts of the human race which appear superfluous,
useless for that goal. For example, the populations of the

76

Third World. A more specific meaning attaches to the choice Nazism made of the European Jews for extermination. I said that this part of the ancient European heritage – Judaic thought – represents a way of thinking entirely turned towards the incessant, interminable listening to and interpretation of a voice. This is what Heidegger's thought, fascinated by the Greek model, completely missed and completely lacked.

(8) As for the voice which prescribes 'You must resist (to the extent that you must think or write)', it of course implies that the problem of the present time is in no way to communicate. What holds the attention and is a question is much rather what this prescription presupposes: what or who is the author (the sender) of this commandment? What is its legitimacy? It is to be thought that this order orders that the question be left open, if it is true that this 'you must' preserves and reserves the coming of the future in its unexpectedness.

6

Newman: The Instant

THE ANGEL

A distinction should be made between the time it takes the
painter to paint the picture (time of 'production'), the time
required to look at and understand the work (time of
'consumption'), the time to which the work refers (a moment,
a scene, a situation, a sequence of events: the time of the
diegetic referent, of the story told by the picture), the time it
takes to reach the viewer once it has been 'created' (the time
of circulation) and finally, perhaps, the time the painting *is*.
This principle, childish as its ambitions may be, should allow
us to isolate different 'sites of time'.

What distinguishes the work of Newman from the corpus
of the 'avant-gardes', and especially from that of American
'abstract expressionism' is not the fact that it is obsessed with
the question of time – an obsession shared by many painters
– but the fact that it gives an unexpected answer to that
question: its answer is that time is the picture itself.

One acceptable way to locate and deploy this paradox is to
compare Newman's site of time with that which governs the
two great works by Duchamp. *The Large Glass* and *Etant
donnés* refer to events, to the 'stripping bare' of the Bride, and
to the discovery of the obscene body. The event of femininity
and the scandal of 'the opposite sex' are one and the same.
Held back in the glass, the event has yet to occur; in the
thicket, behind the peephole, the scandal has already oc-

curred. The two works are two ways of representing the anachronism of the gaze with regard to the event of stripping bare. The 'subject' of the painting is that instant itself, the flash of light which dazzles the eye, an epiphany. But, according to Duchamp, the occurrence of 'femininity' cannot be taken into account *within* the time of the gaze of 'virility'.

It follows that the time it takes to 'consume' (experience, comment upon) these works is, so to speak, infinite: it is taken up by a search for *apparition* itself (the term is Duchamp's), and 'stripping bare' is the sacreligious and sacred analogon of apparition. Apparition means that something that is other occurs. How can the other be figuratively represented? It would have to be identified, but that is contradictory. Duchamp organized the space of the *Bride* according to the principle of 'not yet' and that of *Etant donnés* according to that of 'no longer' Anyone who looks at the Glass is waiting for Godot; the voyeur pursues a fugitive Albertine behind the door of *Etant donnés*. These two works by Duchamp act as a hinge between Proust's impassioned anamnesis and Beckett's parody of looking to the future.

The purpose of a painting by Newman is not to show that duration is in excess of consciousness, but to be the occurrence, the moment which has arrived. There are two differences between Newman and Duchamp, one 'poetic', so to speak, and the other thematic. Duchamp's theme is related, however distantly, to a genre: that of *Vanitas*; Newman's belongs to the Annunciations, the Epiphanies. But the gap between the two plastic poetics is wider than that. A painting by Newman is an angel. It announces nothing; it is in itself the annunciation. Duchamp's great pieces are a plastic gamble, an attempt to outwit the gaze (and the mind) because he is trying to give an analogical representation of how time outwits consciousness. But Newman is not representing a non-representable annunciation; he allows it to present itself.

The time taken to 'consume' a painting by Newman is quite different from the time demanded by Duchamp's great works. One never finishes recounting *The Large Glass* and *Etant donnés*. The Bride is enveloped in the story, or stories, induced by the strange names sketched on the scraps of paper of the Boxes, etched on the glass, represented by commentators. In the instructions provided for the installation of *Etant donnés* narrativity is held back and almost disappears, but it governs the very space of the obscene creche. It tells the story of a nativity. And the baroque nature of the materials demands many a story.

A canvas by Newman draws a contrast between stories and its plastic nudity. Everything is there – dimensions, colours, lines – but there are no allusions. So much so that it is a problem for the commentator. What can one say that is not given? It is not difficult to describe, but the description is as flat as a paraphrase. The best gloss consists of the question: what can one say? Or of the exclamation 'Ah'. Of surprise: 'Look at that.' So many expressions of a feeling which does have a name in the modern aesthetic tradition (and in the work of Newman): the sublime. It is feeling of 'there' (*Voilà*). There is almost nothing to 'consume', or if there is, I do not know what it is. One cannot consume an occurrence, but merely its meaning. The feeling of the instant is instantaneous.

OBLIGATION

Newman's attempt to break with the space of *vedute* affects its 'pragmatic' foundation. He is no longer a painter-prince, an 'I' who displays his glory (or poverty in the case of Duchamp) to a third party (including himself, of course) in accordance with the 'communication. structure' which founded classical modernity. Duchamp works on this structure as best he can, notably by researching multidimensional space and all sorts of 'hinges'. His work as a whole is inscribed in the great temporal hinge between too early/too late. It is always a matter of 'too much', which is an index of poverty, whereas glory, like Cartesian *générosité*, requires respectability. And yet Duchamp is working on a pictorial plastic message which is transmitted from a sender, the painter, to a receiver, the public, and which deals with a referent, a diegesis which the public has difficulty in seeing, but which it is called upon to try to see by the myriad ruses and paradoxes contrived by the painter. The eye explores under the regime of *Guess*.

Newman's space is no longer triadic in the sense of being organized around a sender, a receiver and a referent. The message 'speaks' of nothing; it emanates from no one. It is not Newman who is speaking, or who is using painting to show us something. The message (the painting) is the messenger; it 'says': '*Here I am*', in other words, '*I am yours*' or '*Be mine.*' Two non-substitutable agencies, which exist only in the urgency of the here and now: me, you. The referent (what the painting 'talks about') and the sender (its 'author') have no pertinence, not even a negative pertinence or an allusion to an impossible presence. The message is the presentation, but it presents nothing; it is, that is, presence. This 'pragmatic' organization is much closer to an ethics than to any aesthetics or poetics. Newman is concerned with giving colour, line or rhythm the force of an obligation within a face-to-face relationship, in the second person, and his model cannot be *Look at this (over there)*; it must be *Look at me* or, to be more accurate, *Listen to me*. For obligation is a modality of time rather than of space and its organ is the ear rather than the eye. Newman thus takes to extremes the refutation of the *distinguo* introduced by Lessing's *Laocoon*, a refutation which has of course been the central concern of avant-garde research since, say, Delaunay or Malevitch.

SUBJECT-MATTER

Subject-matter is not, however, eliminated from Newman's painting in any strict sense. In a monologue entitled *The Plasmic Image* (1943–5), Newman stresses the importance of subject-matter in painting. In the absence of subject-matter, he writes, painting becomes 'ornamental'. Moribund as it may be, surrealism has to be given credit for having maintained the need for subject-matter, and for thus preventing the new generation of American painters (Rothko, Gottlieb, Gorky, Pollock, Baziotes) from being seduced by the empty abstraction to which the European schools succumbed after 1910.

If we accept the views of Thomas B. Hess, the 'subject-matter' of Newman's work is 'artistic creation' itself, a

81

symbol of Creation itself, of the Creation story of *Genesis*. One might agree in so far as one can accept a mystery or at least an enigma. In the same monologue Newman writes: 'The subject matter of creation is chaos.' The titles of many of his paintings suggest that they should be interpreted in terms of a (paradoxical) idea of *beginning*. Like a flash of lightning in the darkness or a line on an empty surface, the Word separates, divides, institutes a difference, makes tangible because of that difference, minimal though it may be, and therefore inaugurates, a sensible world. This beginning is an antinomy. It takes place in the world as its initial difference, as the beginning of its history. It does not belong to this world because it begets it, it falls from a prehistory, or from an a-history. The paradox is that of performance, or occurrence. Occurrence is the instant which 'happens', which 'comes' unexpectedly but which, once it is there, takes its place in the network of what has happened. Any instant can be the beginning, provided that it is grasped in terms of its *quod* rather than its *quid*. Without this flash, there would be nothing, or there would be chaos. The flash (like the instant) is always there, and never there. The world never stops beginning. For Newman, creation is not an act performed by someone; it is what happens (this) in the midst of the indeterminate.

If, then, there is any 'subject-matter', it is immediacy. It happens here and now. What [*quid*] happens comes later. The beginning is *that* there is . . . [*quod*]; the world, *what* there is.

Duchamp took as his subject-matter the imperceptibility of the instant, which he tried to represent by using spatial artifices. From *Onement I* (1948) onwards, Newman's work ceases to refer, as though through a screen, to a history which is situated on the other side, even if that history were as stripped down and as supremely symbolic as is, for Duchamp, the discovery, invention or vision of the other (sex). Take the sequence of 'early' paintings (in which Newman becomes Newman), that come flooding after *Onement I: Galaxy, Abraham, The Name, Onement II* (1949), *Joshua, The Name II, Vir Heroicus Sublimis* (1950–1) or the series of five *Untitled* paintings (1950), which ends with *The Wild*, and each of which measures between one and two metres in height and four to five centimetres in breadth; we can see that these works clearly do not 'recount' any event, that they do not refer figuratively to scenes taken from narratives known to the viewer, or which he or she can reconstitute. No doubt they do symbolize events, as their titles suggest. And to a certain extent the titles do lend credence to Hess's Kabbalistic commentaries, as does Newman's known interest in reading the Torah and the Talmud. Yet Hess himself admits that Newman never used his paintings to transmit a message to the viewer, and never illustrated an idea or painted an allegory. Any commentary must be guided by the principle that these works are non-figurative, even in a symbolic sense.

If we examine only the plastic presentation which offers itself to our gaze without the help of the connotations suggested by the titles, we feel not only that we are being held back from giving any interpretation, but that we are being held back from deciphering the painting itself; identifying it on the basis of line, colour, rhythm, format, scale, materials (medium and pigment) and support seems to be easy, almost immediate. It obviously hides no technical secrets, no cleverness that might delay the understanding of our gaze, or that might therefore arouse our curiosity. It is neither seductive nor equivocal; it is clear, 'direct', open and 'poor'.

It has to be admitted that none of these canvases, even if it does belong to a series, has any purpose other than to *be* a visual event in itself (and this is also true, if not more so, of the fourteen *Stations* of 1958–66). The time of what is recounted (the flash of the knife raised against Isaac) and the time taken to recount that time (the corresponding verses of Genesis) cease to be dissociated. They are condensed into the plastic (linear, chromatic, rhythmic) instant that *is* the painting. Hess would say that the painting rises up [*se dresse*], like the appeal from the Lord that stays the hand of Abraham. One might say that, but one might also say in more sober terms that it arises, just as an occurrence arises. The picture presents, being offers itself up in the here and now. No one, and especially not Newman, makes *me* see it in the sense of recounting or interpreting what I see. I (the viewer) am no more than an ear open to the sound which comes to it from out of the silence; the painting is that sound, an accord.

Arising [*se dresser*], which is a constant theme in Newman, must be understood in the sense of pricking up one's ears [*dresser son oreille*], of listening.

THE SUBLIME

The work of Newman belongs to the aesthetic of the sublime, which Boileau introduced via his translation of Longinus, which was slowly elaborated from the end of the seventeenth century onwards in Europe, of which Kant and Burke were the most scrupulous analysts, and which the German idealism of Fichte and Hegel in particular subsumed – thereby misrecognizing it – under the principle that all thought and all reality forms a system. Newman had read Burke. He found him 'a bit surrealist' (cf. the monologue entitled *The Sublime is Now*). And yet in his own way Burke put his finger on an essential feature of Newman's project.

Delight, or the negative pleasure which in contradictory, almost neurotic fashion, characterizes the feeling of the sublime, arises from the removal of the threat of pain. Certain 'objects' and certain 'sensations' are pregnant with a threat to our self-preservation, and Burke refers to that threat as *terror*: shadows, solitude, silence and the approach of death may be 'terrible' in that they announce that the gaze, the other, language or life will soon be extinguished. One feels that it is possible that soon nothing more will take place. What is sublime is the feeling that something will happen, despite everything, within this threatening void, that something will take 'place' and will announce that everything is not over. That place is mere 'here', the most minimal occurrence.

Now Burke attributes to *poetry*, or to what we would now call writing, the twofold and thwarted finality of inspiring terror (or threatening that language will cease, as we would put it) and of meeting the challenge posed by this failure of the word by provoking or accepting the advent of an 'unheard of' phrase. He deems painting incapable of fulfilling this sublime office in its own order. Literature is free to combine words and to experiment with sentences; it has within it an unlimited power, the power of language in all its sufficiency, but in Burke's view the art of painting is hampered by the constraints of figurative representation. With a simple expression like 'The Angel of the Lord', he writes, the poet opens up an infinite number of associations for the mind; no painted image can equal that treasure; it can never be in excess of what the eye can recognize.

We know how surrealist painting tries to get around this inadequacy. It includes the infinite in its compositions. Figurative elements, which are at least defined if not always recognizable, are arranged together in paradoxical fashion (the model is the dream-work). This 'solution' is, however, still vulnerable to Burke's objection that painting has little potential for sublimity: residual fragments of 'perceptive reality' are simply being assembled in a different manner. And Newman finds Burke 'a bit surrealist' because, as a painter, he sees only too well that this condemnation can only apply to an art which insists upon representing, upon making recognizable.

In his *Critique of Judgement* Kant outlines, rapidly and almost without realizing it, another solution to the problem of sublime painting. One cannot, he writes, represent the power of infinite might or absolute magnitude within space and time because they are pure Ideas. But one can at least allude to them, or 'evoke' them by means of what he baptizes a 'negative presentation'. As an example of this paradox of a representation which represents nothing, Kant cites the Mosaic law which forbids the making of graven images. This is only an indication, but it prefigures the Minimalist and abstractionist solutions painting will use to try to escape the figurative prison.

For Newman, the escape does not take the form of transgressing the limits established for figurative space by Renaissance and Baroque art, but of reducing the event-bound time [*temps événementiel*] in which the legendary or historical scene took place to a presentation of the pictorial object itself. It is chromatic matter alone, and its relationship with the material (the canvas, which is sometimes left unprimed) and the lay-out (scale, format, proportions), which must inspire the wonderful surprise, the wonder that there should be something rather than nothing. Chaos threatens, but the flash of the *Tzim-tzum*, the zip, takes places, divides the shadows, breaks down the light into colours like a prism, and arranges them across the surface like a universe. Newman said that he was primarily a draughtsman. There is something holy about line in itself.

'My paintings are concerned neither with the manipulation of space nor with the image, but with the sensation of time', writes Newman in *Prologue for a New Aesthetic*, an unfinished 'monologue' dating from 1949. He adds: 'Not the *sense* of time, which has been the underlying subject matter of painting, which involves feelings of nostalgia or high drama; it is always associative and historical . . .', The manuscript of the *Prologue* breaks off here. But some earlier lines allow us to elaborate further on the time in question.

Newman describes how, in August 1949, he visited the mounds built by the Miami Indians in south-west Ohio, and the Indian fortifications at Newark, Ohio. 'Standing before the Miamisburg mound – surrounded by these simple walls of mud – I was confounded by the absoluteness of the sensation, by their self-evident simplicity.' In a subsequent conversation with Hess, he comments on the event of the sacred site. 'Looking at the site you feel, Here I am, *here* . . . and out beyond there (beyond the limits of the site) there is chaos, nature rivers, landscapes . . . but here you get a sense of your own presence . . . I became involved with the idea of making the viewer present: the idea that "Man is present".'

Hess compares this statement with the text written by Newman in 1963 to introduce a maquette for a synagogue which he designed and built together with Robert Murray for the Recent American Synagogue Architecture exhibition. The synagogue is a perfect 'subject' for the architect; he is not constrained by any spatial organization except in so far as he is required to reinstate as best he can the commandment: 'Know before whom you stand.'

It is a place, Makom, where each man may be called up to stand before the Torah to read his portion . . . My purpose is to create a place, not an environment; to deny the contemplation of the objects of ritual . . . Here in this synagogue, each man sits, private and secluded in the dugouts, waiting to be called, not to ascend a stage, but to go up to the mound where, under the tension of that "Tzim-tzum" that created light and the world, he can experience a total sense of his own personality before the Torah and His Name.

On both the sketches and the plan, the place where the Torah is read is inscribed 'mound'.

This condensation of Indian space and Jewish space has its source and its end in an attempt to capture 'presence'. Presence is the instant which interrupts the chaos of history and which recalls, or simply calls out that 'there is', even before that which is has any signification. It is permissible to call this idea 'mystical', given that it does concern the mystery of being. But being is not meaning. If Newman is to be believed, being procures 'personality' a 'total meaning' by revealing itself instantaneously. An unfortunate expression, in three senses. It so happens that neither signification, totality nor personality are at stake. Those instances come 'after' something has happened, and they do so in order to be situated within that something. *Makom* means place, but that 'place' is also the Biblical name for the Lord. It has to be understood in the sense of 'taking place', in the sense of 'advent'.

PASSION

In 1966 Newman exhibited the fourteen *Stations of the Cross* at the Guggenheim. He gave them the subtitle: *Lama Sabachthani*, the cry of despair uttered by Jesus on the cross: *My God, why hast thou forsaken me?* In a text written to accompany the exhibition, Newman writes: 'This question that has no answer has been with us so long – since Jesus – since Abraham – the original question.' This is the Hebrew version of the Passion: the reconciliation of existence (and therefore of death) and signification does not take place. We are still waiting for the Messiah who will bring meaning. The only 'response' to the question of the abandoned that has ever been heard is not *Know why*, but *Be*. Newman entitled a canvas *Be* and in 1970, the year in which he died, he reworked it as *Be I* (*Second Version*). A second canvas, which was entitled *Resurrection* by the dealer who exhibited it in New York in 1962, was shown together with the *Stations* at the Guggenheim in 1966 under the title *Be II* (it was begun in 1961). In Hess's book, the reproduction of this work bears the legend *First Station, Be II*.

It has to be understood that this *Be* is not concerned with the resurrection in the sense of the Christian mystery, but with the recurrence of a prescription emanating from silence or from the void, and which perpetuates the passion by reiterating it from its beginnings. When we have been abandoned by meaning, the artist has a professional duty to bear witness that *there is*, to respond to the order to be. The painting becomes evidence, and it is fitting that it should not offer anything that has to be deciphered, still less interpreted. Hence the use of flat tints, of non-modulated colours and then the so-called elementary colours of *Who's Afraid of Red Yellow and Blue*? (1966–7). The question mark of the title is that in *Is it happening*?, and the *afraid* must, I think, be taken as an allusion to Burke's terror, to the terror that surrounds the event, the relief that *there is*.

Being announces itself in the imperative. Art is not a genre defined in terms of an end (the pleasure of the addressee), and still less is it a game whose rules have to be discovered; it accomplishes an ontological task, that is, a 'chronological task'. It accomplishes it without completing it. It must constantly begin to testify anew to the occurrence by letting the occurrence be. In Newman's first sculptures of 1963–6, which are entitled *Here I, Here II* and *Here III* and in the *Broken Obelisk* he completed in 1961, we find so many three-dimensional versions of the zip which strikes through all the paintings in a rectilinear slash, ineluctably, but never in the same place. In Newman verticality does not simply connote elation, or being torn away from a land that has been abandoned and from non-meaning. It does not merely rise up; it descends like a thunderbolt. The tip of the inverted obelisk touches the apex of the pyramid, 'just as' the finger of God touches that of Adam on the ceiling of the Sistine Chapel. The work rises up [*se dresse*] in an instant, but the flash of the instant strikes it like a minimal command: *Be*.

7

The Sublime and the Avant-Garde

I

In 1950–1, Barnett Baruch Newman painted a canvas measuring 2.42 m by 5.42 m which he called *Vir Heroicus Sublimis*. In the mid-sixties he entitled his first three sculptures *Here I, Here II, Here III*. Another painting was called *Not Over There, Here*, two paintings were called *Now*, and two others were entitled *Be*. In December 1948, Newman wrote an essay entitled *The Sublime is Now*.

How is one to understand the sublime, or, let us say provisionally, the object of a sublime experience, as a 'here and now'? Quite to the contrary, isn't it essential to this feeling that it alludes to something which can't be shown, or presented (as Kant said, *dargestellt*)? In a short unfinished text dating from late 1949, *Prologue for a New Aesthetic*, Newman wrote that in his painting, he was not concerned with a 'manipulation of space nor with the image, but with a sensation of time'. He added that by this he did not mean time laden with feelings of nostalgia, or drama, or references and history, the usual subjects of painting. After this denial [*dénégation*] the text stops short.

So, what kind of time was Newman concerned with, what 'now' did he have in mind? Thomas B. Hess, his friend and commentator, felt justified in writing that Newman's time was the *Makom* or the *Hamakom* of Hebraic tradition – the *there*, the site, the place, which is one of the names given by

89

the Torah to the Lord, the Unnameable. I do not know enough about *Makom* to know whether this was what Newman had in mind. But then again, who does know enough about *now*? Newman can certainly not have been thinking of the 'present instant', the one that tries to hold itself between the future and the past, and gets devoured by them. This *now* is one of the temporal 'ecstasies' that has been analyzed since Augustine's day and particularly since Edmund Husserl, according to a line of thought that has attempted to constitute time on the basis of consciousness. Newman's *now* which is no more than *now* is a stranger to consciousness and cannot be constituted by it. Rather, it is what dismantles consciousness, what deposes consciousness, it is what consciousness cannot formulate, and even what consciousness forgets in order to constitute itself. What we do not manage to formulate is that something happens, *dass etwas geschieht*. Or rather, and more simply, that it happens ... *dass es geschieht*. Not a major event in the media sense, not even a small event. Just an occurrence.

This isn't a matter of sense or reality bearing upon *what* happens or *what* this might mean. Before asking questions about what it is and about its significance, before the *quid*, it must 'first' so to speak 'happen', *quod*. That it happens 'precedes', so to speak, the question pertaining to what happens. Or rather, the question precedes itself, because 'that it happens' is the question relevant as event, and it 'then' pertains to the event that has just happened. The event happens as a question mark 'before' happening as a question. *It happens* is rather 'in the first place' *is it happening, is this it, is it possible?* Only 'then' is any mark determined by the questioning: is this or that happening, is it this or something else, is it possible that this or that?

An event, an occurrence – what Martin Heidegger called *ein Ereignis* – is infinitely simple, but this simplicity can only be approached through a state of privation. That which we call thought must be disarmed. There is a tradition and an institution of philosophy, of painting, of politics, of literature. These 'disciplines' also have a future in the form of Schools, of programmes, projects and 'trends'. Thought works over what is received, it seeks to reflect on it and overcome it. It seeks to determine what has already been thought, written, painted or socialized in order to determine what hasn't been. We know this process well, it is our daily bread. It is the bread of war, soldiers' biscuit. But this agitation, in the most noble sense of the word (agitation is the word Kant gives to the activity of the mind that has judgement and exercises it), this agitation is only possible if something remains to be determined, something that hasn't yet been determined. One can strive to determine this something by setting up a system, a theory, a programme or a project – and indeed one has to, all the while anticipating that something. One can also enquire about the remainder, and allow the indeterminate to appear as a question-mark.

What all intellectual disciplines and institutions presuppose is that not everything has been said, written down or recorded, that words already heard or pronounced are not the last words. 'After' a sentence, 'after' a colour, comes another sentence, another colour. One doesn't know which, but one thinks one knows if one relies on the rules that permit one sentence to link up with another, one colour with another, rules preserved in precisely those institutions of the past and future that I mentioned. The School, the programme, the project – all proclaim that after this sentence comes that sentence, or at least that one kind of sentence is mandatory, that one kind of sentence is permitted, while another is forbidden. This holds true for painting as much as for the other activities of thought. After one pictorial work, another is necessary, permitted or forbidden. After one colour, this other colour; after this line, that one. There isn't an enormous difference between an avant-garde manifesto and a curriculum at the Ecole des Beaux Arts, if one considers them in the light of this relationship to time. Both are options with respect to what they feel is a good thing to happen subsequently. But both also forget the possibility of nothing happening, of words, colours, forms or sounds not coming; of this sentence being the last, of bread not coming daily. This is the misery that the painter faces with a plastic surface, of the musician with the acoustic surface, the misery the thinker faces with a desert of thought, and so on. Not only faced with the empty canvas or the empty page, at the 'beginning' of the work, but every time something has to be waited for, and thus forms a question at every point of questioning [*point d'interrogation*], at every 'and what now?'

The possibility of nothing happening is often associated with a feeling of anxiety, a term with strong connotations in modern philosphies of existence and of the unconscious. It gives to waiting, if we really mean waiting, a predominantly negative value. But suspense can also be accompanied by pleasure, for instance pleasure in welcoming the unknown, and even by joy, to speak like Baruch Spinoza, the joy obtained by the intensification of being that the event brings with it. This is probably a contradictory feeling. It is at the very least a sign, the question-mark itself, the way in which *it happens* is withheld and announced: *Is it happening?* The question can be modulated in any tone. But the mark of the question is 'now', *now* like the feeling that nothing might happen: the nothingness now.

Between the seventeenth and eighteenth centuries in Europe this contradictory feeling – pleasure and pain, joy and anxiety, exaltation and depression – was christened or re-christened by the name of the *sublime*. It is around this name that the destiny of classical poetics was hazarded and lost; it is in this name that aesthetics asserted its critical rights over art, and that romanticism, in other words, modernity, triumphed.

It remains to the art historian to explain how the word sublime reappeared in the language of a Jewish painter from New York during the forties. The word *sublime* is common currency today to colloquial French to suggest surprise and admiration, somewhat like America's 'great', but the idea connoted by it has belonged (for at least two centuries) to the most rigorous kind of reflection on art. Newman is not unaware of the aesthetic and philosophical stakes with which the word *sublime* is involved. He read Edmund Burke's *Inquiry* and criticized what he saw as Burke's over- 'surrealist' description of the sublime work. Which is as much as to say that, conversely, Newman judged surrealism to be over-reliant on a pre-romantic or romantic approach to indeterminacy. Thus, when he seeks sublimity in the here-and-now he breaks with the eloquence of romantic art but he does not reject its fundamental task, that of bearing pictorial or otherwise expressive witness to the inexpressible. The inexpressible does not reside in an over there, in another word, or another time, but in this: in that (something) happens. In the determination of pictorial art, the indeterminate, the 'it happens' is the paint, the picture. The paint, the picture as occurrence or event, is not expressible, and it is to this that it has to witness.

To be true to this displacement in which consists perhaps the whole of the difference between romanticism and the 'modern' avant-garde, one would have to read *The Sublime is Now* not as *The Sublime is Now* but as *Now the Sublime is Like This*. Not elsewhere, not up there or over there, not earlier or later, not once upon a time. But as here, now, it happens that, . . . and it's this painting. Here and now there is this painting, rather than nothing, and that's what is sublime. Letting go of all grasping intelligence and of its power, disarming it, recognizing that this occurrence of painting was not necessary and is scarcely foreseeable, a privation in the face of *Is it happening?* guarding the occurrence 'before' any defence, any illustration, and any commentary, guarding before being on one's guard, before 'looking' [*regarder*] under the aegis of *now*, this is the rigour of the avant-garde. In the determination of literary art this requirement with respect to the *Is it happening?* found one of its most rigorous realizations in Gertrude Stein's *How to Write*. It's still the sublime in the sense that Burke and Kant described and yet it isn't their sublime any more.

II

I have said that the contradictory feeling with which indeterminacy is both announced and missed was what was at stake in reflection on art from the end of the seventeenth to the end of the eighteenth centuries. The sublime is perhaps the only mode of artistic sensibility to characterize the modern. Paradoxically, it was introduced to literary discussion and vigorously defended by the French writer who has been classified in literary history as one of the most dogged advocates of ancient classicism. In 1674 Boileau published his *Art poétique*, but he also published *Du Sublime*, his translation or transcription from the *Peri tou hupsou*. It is a treatise, or rather an essay, attributed to a certain Longinus about whose identity there has long been confusion, and whose life we now estimate as having begun towards the end of the first century of our era. The author was a rhetorician. Basically, he taught those oratorical devices with which a speaker can persuade or move (depending on the genre) his audience. The didactics of rhetoric had been traditional since Aristotle, Cicero and Quintilian. They were linked to the republican institution; one had to know how to speak before assemblies and tribunals.

One might expect that Longinus' text would invoke the maxims and advice transmitted by this tradition by perpetuating the didactic form of *techne rhetorike*. But surprisingly, the sublime, the indeterminate, were destabilizing the text's didactic intention. I cannot analyze this uncertainty here. Boileau himself and numerous other commentators, especially Fénélon, were aware of it and concluded that the sublime could only be discussed in sublime style. Longinus certainly tried to define sublimity in discourse, writing that it was unforgettable, irresistible, and most important, thought-provoking – '*il y a à partir d'elle beaucoup de réflexion*' [*hou polle anatheoresis*] [from the sublime springs a lot of reflection]. He also tried to locate sources for the sublime in the ethos of rhetoric, in its pathos, in its techniques: figures of speech, diction, enunciation, composition. He sought in this way to bend himself to the rules of the genre of the 'treatise' (whether of rhetoric or poetics, or politics) destined to be a model for practitioners.

However, when it comes to the sublime, major obstacles get in the way of a regular exposition of rhetorical or poetic principles. There is, for example, wrote Longinus, a sublimity of thought sometimes recognizable in speech by its extreme simplicity of turn of phrase, at the precise point where the high character of the speaker makes one expect greater solemnity. It sometimes even takes the form of outright silence. I don't mind if this simplicity, this silence, is taken to be yet another rhetorical figure. But it must be granted that it constitutes the most indeterminate of figures. What can remain of rhetoric (or of poetics) when the rhetorician in Boileau's translation announces that to attain the sublime effect 'there is no better figure of speech than one which is completely hidden, that which we do not even recognize as a figure of speech?' Must we admit that there are techniques for hiding figures, that there are figures for the erasure of figures? How do we distinguish between a hidden figure and what is not a figure? And what is it, if it isn't a figure? And what about this, which seems to be a major blow to didactics: when it is sublime, discourse accommodates defects, lack of taste, and formal imperfections. Plato's style, for example, is full of bombast and bloated strained comparisons. Plato, in short, is a mannerist, or a baroque writer compared to a Lysias, and so is Sophocles compared to an Ion, or Pindar compared to a Bacchylides. The fact remains that, like those first named, he is sublime, whereas the second ones are merely perfect. Shortcomings in technique are therefore trifling matters if they are the price to be paid for 'true grandeur'. Grandeur in speech is true when it bears witness to the incommensurability between thought and the real world.

Is it Boileau's transcription that suggests this analogy, or is it the influence of early Christianity on Longinus? The fact that grandeur of spirit it not of this world cannot but suggest Pascal's hierarchy of orders. The kind of perfection that can be demanded in the domain of *techne* isn't necessarily a desirable attribute when it comes to sublime feeling. Longinus even goes so far as to propose inversions of reputedly natural and rational syntax as examples of sublime effect. As for Boileau, in the preface he wrote in 1674 for Longinus' text, in still further addenda made in 1683 and 1701 and also in the *Xth Réflexion* published in 1710 after his death he makes final the previous tentative break with the classical institution of *techne*. The sublime, he says, cannot be taught, and didactics are thus powerless in this respect; the sublime is not linked to rules that can be determined through poetics; the sublime only requires that the reader or listener have conceptual range, taste and the ability 'to sense what everyone senses first'. Boileau therefore takes the same stand as Père Bouhours, when in 1671 the latter declared that beauty demands more than just a respect for rules, that it requires a further 'je ne sais quoi', also called *genius* or something 'incomprehensible and inexplicable', a 'gift from God', a fundamentally 'hidden' phenomenon that can be recognized only by its effects on the addressee. And in the polemic that set him against Pierre-Daniel Huet, over the issue of whether the Bible's *Fiat Lux, et Lux fuit* is sublime, as Longinus thought it was, Boileau refers to the opinion of the Messieurs de Port Royal and in particular to Silvestre de Saci: the Jansenists are masters when it comes to matters of hidden meaning, of eloquent silence, of feeling that transcends all reason and finally of openness to the *Is it happening?*

At stake in these poetic-theological debates is the status of works of art. Are they copies of some ideal model? Can reflection on the more 'perfect' examples yield rules of formation that determine their success in achieving what they want, that is, persuasiveness and pleasure? Can understanding suffice for this kind of reflection? By meditating on the theme of sublimity and of indeterminacy, meditation about works of art imposes a major change on *techne* and the institutions linked to it – Academies, Schools, masters and disciples, taste, the enlightened public made up of princes and courtiers. It is the very destination or destiny of works which is being questioned. The predominance of the idea of *techne* placed works under a multiple regulation, that of the model taught in the studios, Schools and Academies, that of the taste shared by the aristocratic public, that of a purposiveness of art, which was to illustrate the glory of a name, divine or human, to which was linked the perfection of some cardinal virtue or other. The idea of the sublime disrupts this harmony. Let us magnify the features of this disruption. Under Diderot's pen, *techne* becomes *'le petit technique'* (mere trivial technique). The artist ceases to be guided by a culture which made of him the sender and master of a message of glory: he becomes, in so far as he is a genius, the involuntary addressee of an inspiration come to him from an 'I know not what.' The public no longer judges according to the criteria of a taste ruled by the tradition of shared pleasure: individuals unknown to the artist (the 'people') read books, go through the galleries of the Salons, crowd into the theatres and the public concerts, they are prey to unforeseeable feelings: they are shocked, admiring, scornful, indifferent. The question is not that of pleasing them by leading them to identify with a name and to participate in the glorification of its virtue, but that of surprising them. 'The sublime', writes Boileau, 'is not strictly speaking something which is proven or demonstrated, but a marvel, which seizes one, strikes one, and makes one feel.' The very imperfections, the distortions of taste, even ugliness, have their share in the shock-effect. Art does not imitate nature, it creates a world apart, *eine Zwischenwelt*, as Paul Klee will say; *eine Nebenwelt*, one might say in which the monstrous and the formless have their rights because they can be sublime.

You will (I hope) excuse such a simplication of the transformation which takes place with the modern development of the idea of the sublime. The trace of it could be found before modern times, in medieval aesthetics – that of the Victorines for example. In any case, it explains why reflection on art should no longer bear essentially on the 'sender' instance/agency of works, but on the 'addressee' instance. And under the name 'genius' the latter instance is situated, not only on the side of the public, but also on the side of the artist, a feeling which he does not master. Henceforth it seems right to analyze the ways in which the subject is affected, its ways of receiving and experiencing feelings, its ways of judging works. This is how aesthetics, the analysis of the addressee's feelings, comes to supplant poetics and rhetoric, which are didactic forms, of and by the understanding, intended for the artist as sender. No longer 'How does one make a work of art?', but 'What is it to experience an affect proper to art?' And indeterminacy returns, even within the analysis of this last question.

III

Baumgarten published his *Aesthetica*, the first aesthetics, in 1750. Kant would say of this work simply that it was based on an error. Baumgarten confuses judgement, in its determinant usage, when the understanding organizes phenomena according to categories, with judgement in its reflexive usage when, in the form of feeling, it relates to the indeterminate relationship between the faculties of the judging subject. Baumgarten's aesthetics remains dependent on a conceptually determined relationship to the work of art. The sense of beauty is for Kant, on the contrary, kindled by a free harmony between the function of images and the function of concepts occasioned by an object of art or nature. The aesthetics of the sublime is still more indeterminate: a pleasure mixed with pain, a pleasure that comes from pain. In the event of an absolutely large object – the desert, a mountain, a pyramid – or one that is absolutely powerful – a storm at sea, an erupting volcano – which like all absolutes can only be thought, without any sensible/sensory intuition, as an Idea of reason, the faculty of presentation, the imagination, fails to provide a representation corresponding to this Idea. This failure of expression gives rise to a pain, a kind of cleavage within the subject between what can be conceived and what can be imagined or presented. But this pain in turn engenders a pleasure, in fact a double pleasure: the impotence of the imagination attests *a contrario* to an imagination striving to figure even that which cannot be figured, and that imagination thus aims to harmonize its object with that of reason – and that furthermore the inadequacy of the images is a negative sign of the immense power of ideas. This dislocation of the faculties among themselves gives rise to the extreme tension (Kant calls it agitation) that characterizes the pathos of the sublime, as opposed to the calm feeling of beauty. At the edge of the break, infinity, or the absoluteness of the Idea can be revealed in what Kant calls a negative presentation, or even a non-presentation. He cites the Jewish law banning images as an eminent example of negative presentation: optical pleasure when reduced to near nothingness promotes an infinite contemplation of infinity. Even before romantic art had freed itself from classical and baroque figuration, the door had thus been opened to enquiries pointing towards abstract and Minimal art. Avant-gardism is thus present in germ in the Kantian aesthetic of the sublime. However, the art whose

98

effects are analyzed in that aesthetics is, of course, essentially made up of attempts to represent sublime objects. And the question of time, of the *Is it happening?*, does not form part – at least not explicitly – of Kant's problematic.

I do, however, believe that question to be at the centre of Edmund Burke's *Philosophical Inquiry into the Origin of our Ideas of the Sublime and Beautiful*, published in 1757. Kant may well reject Burke's thesis as empiricism and physiologism, he may well borrow from Burke the analysis of the characterizing contradiction of the feeling of the sublime, but he strips Burke's aesthetic of what I consider to be its major stake – to show that the sublime is kindled by the threat of nothing further happening. Beauty gives a positive pleasure. But there is another kind of pleasure that is bound to a passion stronger than satisfaction, and that is pain and impending death. In pain the body affects the soul. But the soul can also affect the body as though it were experiencing some externally induced pain, by the sole means of representations that are unconsciously associated with painful situations. This entirely spiritual passion, in Burke's lexicon, is called terror. Terrors are linked to privation: privation of light, terror of darkness; privation of others, terror of solitude; privation of language, terror of silence; privation of objects, terror of emptiness; privation of life, terror of death. What is terrifying is that the *It happens that* does not happen, that it stops happening.

Burke wrote that for this terror to mingle with pleasure and with it to produce the feeling of the sublime, it is also necessary that the terror-causing threat be suspended, kept at bay, held back. This suspense, this lessening of a threat or a danger, provokes a kind of pleasure that is certainly not that of a positive satisfaction, but is, rather, that of relief. This is still a privation, but it is privation at one remove; the soul is deprived of the threat of being deprived of light, language, life. Burke distinguishes this pleasure of secondary privation from positive pleasures, and he baptizes it with the name *delight*.

Here then is an account of the sublime feeling: a very big, very powerful object threatens to deprive the soul of any 'it happens', strikes it with 'astonishment' (at lower intensities the soul is seized with admiration, veneration, respect). The soul is thus dumb, immobilized, as good as dead. Art, by distancing this menace, procures a pleasure of relief, of delight. Thanks to art, the soul is returned to the agitated zone between life and death, and this agitation is its health and its life. For Burke, the sublime was no longer a matter of elevation (the category by which Aristotle defined tragedy), but a matter of intensification.

Another of Burke's observations merits attention because it heralds the possibility of emancipating works of art from the classical rule of imitation. In the long debate over the relative merits of painting and poetry, Burke sides with poetry. Painting is doomed to imitate models, and to figurative representations of them. But if the object of art is to create intense feelings in the addressee of works, figuration by means of images is a limiting constraint on the power of emotive expression since it works by recognition. In the arts of language, particularly in poetry, which Burke considered to be not a genre with rules, but the field where certain researches into language have free rein, the power to move is free from the verisimilitudes of figuration. 'What does one do when one wants to represent an angel in a painting? One paints a beautiful young man with wings: but will painting ever provide anything as great as the addition of this one word – the Angel of the *Lord*? and how does one go about painting, with equal strength of feeling, the words "A universe of death" where ends the journey of the fallen angels in Milton's *Paradise Lost*?'

Words enjoy several privileges when it comes to expressing feelings: they are themselves charged with passionate connotations; they can evoke matters of the soul without having to consider whether they are visible; finally, Burke adds, 'It is in our power to effect with words combinations that would be impossible by any other means.' The arts, whatever their materials, pressed forward by the aesthetics of the sublime in search of intense effects, can and must give up the imitation of models that are merely beautiful, and try out surprising, strange, shocking combinations. Shock is, *par excellence*, the evidence of (something) *happening*, rather than nothing, suspended privation.

Burke's analyses can easily, as you will have guessed, be resumed and elaborated in a Freudian-Lacanian problematic (as Pierre Kaufman and Baldine Saint-Girons have done). But I recall them in a different spirit, the one my subject – the avant-garde – demands. I have tried to suggest that at the dawn of romanticism, Burke's elaboration of the aesthetics of the sublime, and to a lesser degree Kant's, outlined a world of possibilities for artistic experiments in which the avant-gardes would later trace out their paths. There are in general no direct influences, no empirically observable connections. Manet, Cézanne, Braque and Picasso probably did not read Kant or Burke. It is more a matter of an irreversible deviation in the destination of art, a deviation affecting all the valencies of the artistic condition. The artist attempts combinations allowing the event. The art-lover does not experience a simple pleasure, or derive some ethical benefit from his contact with art, but expects an intensification of his conceptual and emotional capacity, an ambivalent enjoyment. Intensity is associated with an ontological dislocation. The art-object no longer bends itself to models, but tries to present the fact that there is an unpresentable; it no longer imitates nature, but is, in Burke, the actualization of a figure potentially there in language. The social community no longer recognizes itself in art-objects, but ignores them, rejects them as incomprehensible, and only later allows the intellectual avant-garde to preserve them in museums as the traces of offensives that bear witness to the power, and the privation, of the spirit.

IV

With the advent of the aesthetics of the sublime, the stake of art in the nineteenth and twentieth centuries was to be the witness to the fact that there is indeterminacy. For painting, the paradox that Burke signalled in his observations on the power of words is, that such testimony can only be achieved in a determined fashion. Support, frame, line, colour, space, the figure – were to remain, in romantic art, subject to the constraint of representation. But this contradiction of end and means had, as early as Manet and Cézanne, the effect of casting doubt on certain rules that had determined, since the Quattrocento, the representation of the figure in space and the organization of colours and values. Reading Cézanne's correspondence, one understands that his *oeuvre* was not that of a talented painter finding his 'style', but that of an artist attempting to respond to the question: what is a painting? His work had at stake to inscribe on the supporting canvas only those 'colouristic sensations', those 'little sensations' that of themselves, according to Cézanne's hypothesis, constitute the entire pictorial existence of objects, fruit, mountain, face, flower, without consideration of either history or 'subject', or line, or space, or even light. These elementary sensations are hidden in ordinary perception which remains under the hegemony of habitual or classical ways of looking. They are only accessible to the painter, and can therefore only be re-established by him, at the expense of an interior ascesis that rids perceptual and mental fields of prejudices inscribed even in vision itself. If the viewer does not submit to a complementary ascesis, the painting will remain senseless and impenetrable to him. The painter must not hesitate to run the risk of being taken to be a mere dauber. 'One paints for very few people', writes Cézanne. Recognition from the regulatory institutions of painting – Academy, salons, criticism, taste – is of little importance compared to the judgement made by the painter-researcher and his peers on the success obtained by the work of art in relation to what is really at stake: to make seen what makes one see, and not what is visible.

Maurice Merleau-Ponty elaborated on what he rightly called 'Cézanne's doubt' as though what was at stake for the painter was indeed to grasp and render perception at its birth – perception 'before' perception. I would say: colour in its occurrence, the wonder that 'it happens' ('it', something: colour), at least to the eye. There is some credulity on the part of the phenomenologist in this trust he places in the 'originary' value of Cézanne's 'little sensations'. The painter himself, who often complained of their inadequacy, wrote that they were 'abstractions', that 'they did not suffice for covering the canvas'. But why should it be necessary to cover the canvas? Is it forbidden to be abstract?

The doubt which gnaws at the avant-gardes did not stop with Cézanne's 'colouristic sensations' as though they were indubitable, and, for that matter, no more did it stop with the abstractions they heralded. The task of having to bear witness to the indeterminate carries away, one after another, the barriers set up by the writings of theorists and by the manifestos of the painters themselves. A formalist definition of the pictorial object, such as that proposed in 1961 by Clement Greenberg when confronted with American 'post-plastic' abstraction, was soon overturned by the current of Minimalism. Do we have to have stretchers so that the canvas is taut? No. What about colours? Malevitch's black square on white had already answered this question in 1915. Is an object necessary? Body art and happenings went about proving that it is not. A space, at least, a space in which to display, as Duchamp's 'fountain' still suggested? Daniel Buren's work testifies to the fact that even this is subject to doubt.

Whether or not they belong to the current that art history calls Minimalism or *arte povera*, the investigations of the avant-gardes question one by one the constituents one might have thought 'elementary' or at the 'origin' of the art of painting. They operate *ex minimis*. One would have to confront the demand for rigour that animates them with the principle sketched out by Adorno at the end of *Negative Dialectics*, and that controls the writing of his *Aesthetic Theory*: the thought that 'accompanies metaphysics in its fall', he said, can only proceed in terms of 'micrologies'.

Micrology is not just metaphysics in crumbs, any more than Newman's painting is Delacroix in scaps. Micrology inscribes the occurrence of a thought as the unthought that remains to be thought in the decline of 'great' philosophical thought. The avant-gardist attempt inscribes the occurrence of a sensory now as what cannot be presented and which remains to be presented in the decline of great representa-tional painting. Like micrology, the avant-garde is not concerned with what happens to the 'subject', but with: 'Does it happen?', with privation. This is the sense in which it still belongs to the aesthetics of the sublime.

103

In asking questions of the *It happens* that the work of art is, avant-garde art abandons the role of identification that the work previously played in relation to the community of addressees. Even when conceived, as it was by Kant, as a *de jure* horizon or presumption rather than a *de facto* reality, a *sensus communis* (which, moreover, Kant refers to only when writing about beauty, not the sublime) does not manage to achieve stability when it comes to interrogative works of art. It barely coalesces, too late, when these works, deposited in museums, are considered part of the community heritage and are made available for its culture and pleasure. And even here, they must be objects, or they must tolerate objectification, for example through photography.

In this situation of isolation and misunderstanding, avant-garde art is vulnerable and subject to repression. It seems only to aggravate the identity-crisis that communities went through during the long 'depression' that lasted from the thirties until the end of 'reconstruction' in the mid-fifties. It is impossible here even to suggest how the Party-states born of fear faced with the 'Who are we?', and the anxiety of the void, tried to convert this fear or anxiety into hatred of the avant-gardes. Hildegarde Brenner's study of artistic policy under Nazism, or the films of Hans-Jürgen Syberberg do not merely analyze these repressive manoeuvres. They also explain how neo-romantic, neo-classical and symbolic forms imposed by the cultural commissars and collaborationist artists – painters and musicians especially – had to block the negative dialectic of the *Is it happening*?, by translating and betraying the question as a waiting for some fabulous subject or identity: 'Is the pure people coming?', 'Is the Führer coming?', 'Is Siegfried coming?' The aesthetics of the sublime, thus neutralized and converted into a politics of myth, was able to come and build its architectures of human 'formations' on the Zeppelin Feld in Nürnberg.

Thanks to the 'crisis of overcapitalization' that most of today's so-called highly developed societies are going through, another attack on the avant-gardes is coming to light. The threat exerted against the avant-garde search for the artwork event, against attempts to welcome the *now*, no longer requires Party-states to be effective. It proceeds 'directly' out of market economics. The correlation between this and the aesthetics of the sublime is ambiguous, even perverse. The latter, no doubt, has been and continues to be a reaction against the matter-of-fact positivism and the calculated realism that governs the former, as writers on art such as Stendhal, Baudelaire, Mallarmé, Apollinaire and Breton all emphasize.

Yet there is a kind of collusion between capital and the avant-garde. The force of scepticism and even of destruction that capitalism has brought into play, and that Marx never ceased analyzing and identifying, in some way encourages among artists a mistrust of established rules and a willingness to experiment with means of expression, with styles, with ever-new materials. There is something of the sublime in capitalist economy. It is not academic, it is not physiocratic, it admits of no nature. It is, in a sense, an economy regulated by an Idea – infinite wealth or power. It does not manage to present any example from reality to verify this Idea. In making science subordinate to itself through technologies, especially those of language, it only succeeds, on the contrary, in making reality increasingly ungraspable, subject to doubt, unsteady.

The experience of the human subject – individual and collective – and the aura that surrounds this experience, are being dissolved into the calculation of profitability, the satisfaction of needs, self-affirmation through success. Even the virtually theological depth of the worker's condition, and of work, that marked the socialist and union movements for over a century, is becoming devalorized, as work becomes a control and manipulation of information. These observations are banal, but what merits attention is the disappearance of the temporal continuum through which the experience of generations used to be transmitted. The availability of information is becoming the only criterion of social importance. Now information is by definition a short-lived element. As soon as it is transmitted and shared, it ceases to be information, it becomes an environmental given, and 'all is said', we 'know'. It is put into the machine memory. The length of time it occupies is, so to speak, instantaneous. Between two pieces of information, 'nothing happens', by

105

definition. A confusion thereby becomes possible, between what is of interest to information and the director, and what is the question of the avant-gardes, between what happens – the new – and the *Is it happening?*, the *now*.

It is understandable that the art-market, subject like all markets to the rule of the new, can exert a kind of seduction on artists. This attraction is not due to corruption alone. It exerts itself thanks to a confusion between innovation and the *Ereignis*, a confusion maintained by the temporality specific to contemporary capitalism. 'Strong' information, if one can call it that, exists in inverse proportion to the meaning that can be attributed to it in the code available to its receiver. It is like 'noise'. It is easy for the public and for artists, advised by intermediaries – the diffusers of cultural merchandise – to draw from this observation the principle that a work of art is avant-garde in direct proportion to the extent that it is stripped of meaning. Is it not then like an event?

It is still necessary that its absurdity does not discourage buyers, just as the innovation introduced into a commodity must allow itself to be approached, appreciated and purchased by the consumers. The secret of an artistic success, like that of a commercial success, resides in the balance between what is surprising and what is 'well-known', between information and code. This is how innovation in art operates: one re-uses formulae confirmed by previous success, one throws them off-balance by combining them with other, in principle incompatible, formulae, by amalgamations, quotations ornamentations, pastiche. One can go as far as kitsch or the grotesque. One flatters the 'taste' of a public that can have no taste, and the eclecticism or a sensibility enfeebled by the multiplication of available forms and objects. In this way one thinks that one is expressing the spirit of the times, whereas one is merely reflecting the spirit of the market. Sublimity is no longer in art, but in speculation on art.

The enigma of the *Is it happening?* is not dissolved for all this, nor is the task of painting, that there is something which is not determinable, the *There is* [*Il y a*] itself, out of date. The occurrence, the *Ereignis*, has nothing to do with the *petit frisson*, the cheap thrill, the profitable pathos, that accompanies an innovation. Hidden in the cynicism of innovation is certainly the despair that nothing further will happen. But innovating means to behave as though lots of things happened, and to make them happen. Through innovation, the will affirms its hegemony over time. It thus conforms to the metaphysics of capital, which is a technology of time. The innovation 'works'. The question mark of the *Is it happening?*' stops. With the occurrence, the will is defeated. The avant-gardist task remains that of undoing the presumption of the mind with respect to time. The sublime feeling is the name of this privation.

8

Something like:
'Communication . . . without
Communication'

With a view to dramatizing the question laid down, 'Art and Communication', I would just like to recall the regime of representation which is proper, or which has been thought proper, at least since Kant, to aesthetic reception; and, in order to pick out this regime, I will just quote two sentences, aphorisms, which appear to contradict one another perfectly:

> No work of art should be described or explained through the categories of communication.

> One could even define taste as the faculty of judging what renders our feeling, proceeding from a given representation, universally *communicable* without the mediation of a concept.

The first is from Theodore Adorno (*Aesthetic Theory*), the second from Immanuel Kant (*Critique of Judgement*, § 40).

These two aphorisms appear to be contradictory, one saying that art has nothing to do with communication, and the other that the reception of art presupposes and demands a universal communicability without concept. The philosopher is used to contrary theses. The Adorno passage is one of the objections he makes to the Hegelian reduction of the work to the dialectic of the concept. Adorno, not without premonition, discerns in Hegelian thought the beginnings of something like a *communicationalist* ideology, and probably – here

we come back to Kant's formulation – for the very reason
that in Hegel's speculative philosophy there is an absolute
hegemony of the concept. Now in what Adorno calls *communication*, the idea is also implicitly required that if there is
a communication in art and through art, it must be without
concept. So much so, that in spite of the apparent contradiction, Adorno is at this point inserting himself into a tradition
of thinking about art which we get from Kant. There is a
thinking about art which is not a thinking of non-
communication but of non-conceptual communication.

The question I want to dramatize is this: what about
communication without concept at a time when, precisely,
the 'products' of technologies applied to art cannot occur
without the massive and hegemonic intervention of the
concept? In the conflict surrounding the word *communication*, it is understood that the work, or at any rate anything
which is received as art, induces a feeling – before inducing
an understanding – which, constitutively and therefore immediately, is universally communicable, by definition. Such a
feeling is thereby distinguishable from a merely subjective
preference. This communicability, as a demand and not as a
fact, precisely because it is assumed to be originary, *ontological*, eludes communicational activity, which is not a receptiveness but something which is managed, which is done.
This, in my view, is what governs our problematic of 'new
technologies and art', or, put differently, 'art and postmodernity'. This communicability, as it is developed in the Kantian
analysis of the beautiful, is well and truly 'anterior' to
communication in the sense of 'theories of communication',
which include communicative pragmatics (*pragma* is the
same thing as *Handeln*). This assumed communicability,
which takes place immediately in the feeling of the beautiful,
is always presupposed in any conceptual communication.

By showing that the feeling of beauty differs from the other
affects or affections with which it is tempting to confuse it,
including the feeling of sublimity, Kant signifies that it *must*
be *made transitive* immediately, without which there is no
feeling of beauty. The requirement that there be such an
assenting, universal in principle, is constitutive of aesthetic
judgement. So if we keep to a psychological or social or

pragmatic or generally anthropological kind of description, we give up on according to art a specific status as to its reception, and basically, we grant that there is no art. If we abandon this transitivity – potential, immediate, capable of being demanded in the judgement of taste and, simultaneously, demanded in order for there to be art – by the same token we abandon the idea of a community deriving from what Kant calls *sensus communis*, which is to say from an immediately communicable *sentimentality*.

And it cannot be said of a feeling that it must gather everyone's agreement without mediation, im-mediately, without presupposing a sort of *community of feeling* such that every one of the individuals, placed before the same situation, the same work, can at least dispose of an identical judgement without elaborating it conceptually. In the analysis of aesthetic feeling, there is thus also an issue of the analysis of what goes on with a community in general. In the reception of works of art, what is involved is the status of a sentimental, aesthetic community, one certainly 'anterior' to all communication and all pragmatics. The cutting out of intersubjective relations has not yet happened and there would be an assenting, a unanimity possible and capable of being demanded, within an order which cannot 'yet' be that of argumentation between rational and speaking subjects.

The hypothesis of another type of community thus emerges, irreducible to theories of communication. If we accept that assumed communicability is included in the singular aesthetic feeling, and if we accept that this singular aesthetic feeling is the im-mediate mode, which is no doubt to say the poorest and the purest, of a possibility to space and time, necessary forms of *aesthesis*, then can this communicability persist when the forms which should be its occasion are conceptually determined, whether in their generation or in their transmission? What happens to aesthetic feeling when *calculated* situations are put forward as aesthetic?

The opposition between linear system and figurative system indicated in the conference's rubric, not to mention the hopes invested in the calculated production of figures, seems to me irrelevant in relation to the one I am trying to state between *passibility* and activity. Passibility as the possibility of experiencing (*pathos*) presupposes a donation. If we are in a state of passibility, it's that something is happening to us, and when this passibility has a fundamental status, the donation itself is something fundamental, originary. What happens to us is not at all something we have first controlled, programmed, grasped by a concept [*Begriff*]. Or else, if what we are passible to has first been plotted conceptually, how can it *seize us*? How can it test us if we already know, or if we can know – of what, with what, for what, it is done? Or else, if such a feeling, in the very radical sense that Kant tries to give this term, takes place, it must be admitted that what happens to us disconcerts us. When Kant speaks of the *matter* of sensation, which he opposes to its form, its formation, it is precisely to do with what we cannot calculate. We have nothing to say about what it is that administers this matter to us, gives it to us. We cannot conceptualize this sort of *Other* with a capital O which Kant calls a big X. It must certainly be granted that the donation proceeds from an X, which Heidegger called *Being*. This donation which is experienced before (or better, *in*) any capture or conceptualization *gives matter* for reflection, for the conception, and it is *on it*, for it, that we are going to construct our aesthetic philosophy and our theories of communication. There does have to be something which is given first. The feeling is the immediate *welcoming* of what is given. Works produced by the new *techne* necessarily, and to quite diverse degrees, and in diverse parts of themselves, bear the traces of having been determined to be one or more *calculations*, whether in their constitution and/or their restitution, or only in their distribution. And by 'calculation' I don't only mean the kind that occupies the time of computer engineers, but also taking in the inevitable measurability of spaces and times, of all the times, including those dubbed 'working' times, expended in the production of these works and their distrution.

Any industrial reproduction pays homage to this profound and fundamental problematic of *re*-presentation, and aesthetic feeling presupposes something which necessarily is implied, and forgotten, in representation: *presentation*, the fact that something is *there now*. All representations presuppose space and time as that by and in which something happens to us and which is always here and now: the place and the moment. It has to do not with concepts but simply with modes of presentation. As soon as we are within the arts of representation, the question of the here-and-now is hidden. How can there be an *aesthetic* feeling issuing from calculated *re*-presentation alone? How could the traces of the conceptual determination of the forms proposed by the new *techne* leave free the play of reflexive judgement which constitutes aesthetic pleasure? How could the communicability constitutive of this pleasure, which remains potential, promised and not affected, not be excluded by the conceptual, argumentative and techno-scientific – 'realistic' – determination of what is communicated in the product of these new technologies?

In urging this strange problematic of aesthetic feeling in Kant, in its im-mediacy *and* its demand for universal communicability, without which it's not art we're dealing with, I only mean to suggest the following hypothesis: what is hit first of all, and complains, in our modernity, or our postmodernity, is perhaps space and time. What is attacked would be space and time as forms of the donation of what happens. The real 'crisis of foundations' was doubtless not that of the foundations of reason but of any scientific enterprise bearing on so-called real objects, in other words given in sensory space and time.

There are already two aesthetics in Kant, two senses of the word *aesthetic*. In the first Aesthetic (*Critique of Pure Reason*), the question posed is restricted to the elaboration of the sensible (its 'synthesis') through which it is knowable by concept. How is it that concepts can find application in reality? It must be that there are already, in the sensible as it is given to us, types of syntheses of elements, sensible unities, which prepare it for its being taken into intelligibility under concepts. There is an affinity between what is given in the sensible and what the concept is going to do with it. For example in the temporal series of sounds, there is what permits the application of the numerical series. It is this first synthesis which Kant calls *schema* and which, in the sensible, prepares for the conceptual application. We can know the sensible because it has an affinity with the intelligence. In the third Critique, the Aesthetic elaborates the question of

112

the forms. The object at this point is not to understand how science is possible but to understand how it is that in the here-and-now of donation a feeling is produced such that it is only the affective transcription of the forms which float freely in space and time. Kant attributes this feeling to the inscription on the subject of the forms attributable to the productive imagination. The syntheses which take place in the sensible are no longer conceived here by Kant as preparing for science but as permitting *feeling* which is itself preparatory to all knowledge. It is the way that the forms are received by a subject which interests him; he also calls them *monograms*.

There is thus first of all this schema/form problem, but there is further the division of the apprehension of the forms into two aesthetic feelings: the feeling of the beautiful and the feeling of the sublime. This last, whose Analytic Kant introduces without any sort of justification, contrary to rule, has the interesting property of including no im-mediate communicability. The feeling of the sublime is manifested when the presentation of free forms is lacking. It is compatible with the form-less. It is even when the imagination which presents forms finds itself lacking that such a feeling appears. And this latter must go via the *mediation* of an Idea of reason which is the Idea of freedom. We find sublime those spectacles which exceed any real presentation of a form, in other words where what is signified is the superiority of our power of freedom *vis-à-vis* the one manifested in the spectacle itself. In singling out the sublime, Kant places the accent on something directly related to the problem of the failing of space and time. The free-floating forms which aroused the feeling of the beautiful come to be lacking. In a certain way the question of the sublime is closely linked to what Heidegger calls the retreat of Being, retreat of donation. For Heidegger, the welcome accorded something sensory, in other words some meaning embodied in the here-and-now before any concept, no longer has place and moment. This retreat signifies our current fate.

In *The Principle of Reason* and *The Age of the World-Picture*, the opposition is at its greatest between the poetic, receptivity in the sense of this Kantian sentimentality, and the *Gestell* [untranslatable: enframing?], which is to be credited to techno-science. For Heidegger, techno-science at its height was nuclear science; we have done much better in *Gestell* nowadays. It is clear that the in-stallation [same 'root' as *stellen*] of the concept as far as space-time is infinitely more fine in the new technologies than it was in what Heidegger was familiar with. Opposition between two forms of reception: on one side the poetic form which he imputes to the Greeks, and on the other techno-scientific reception (it is still an ontological reception) which occurs under the general regime of the principle of reason and whose explicit birth he sees in Leibniz's thought. It is clear that the idea of the combinatory, and thus of all that governs computer science and communication, is one of the things whose birth is in this, including the infinitesimal.

This problematic should be taken up again, revised and corrected: it seems to me central in the question of 'art and communication'. In Hölderlin's *Remarks* on Oedipus, which it would be necessary for us to ponder, the poet notes that the true tragedy of Oedipus is that the god has categorically turned away from man. The real tragedy is not *Oedipus Tyrannos* (the plot, the murder, the misunderstanding) but *Oedipus at Colonus*, in other words when fate is accomplished and nothing more happens to the hero, nothing is destined for him any more. The loss of all destiny is the essential feature of the drama and in this 'nothing happens' also lies the essential feature of our problematic. It is clear that what is called communication is always, in every case, that nothing happens, that we are not destined. And in this connection Hölderlin adds this quite remarkable sentence: 'At the extreme limit of distress, there is in fact nothing left but the conditions of time and space.'

At the horizon of what is called the 'end of art', which Hegelian though discovers at the start of the nineteenth century, we find the melancholy of 'there is nothing left but the conditions of time and space', which tends and bandages itself in that immense work of mourning, that immense remission which is Hegelian dialectical thought. Not only is it going to be necessary to absorb the fact that 'there is nothing left but time and space' as pure conditions (which is done from the start of the first great work, the *Phenomenology of Spirit*, where it is demonstrated that space and time have their truth not in themselves but in the concept, that there is no here-and-now, that the sensible is always already mediated by the understanding), but the theme of the end of art reveals on another level the persistence of the theme of the retreat of the donation and the crisis of the aesthetic. If there is no time, if time is the concept, there is no art except by mistake, or rather the moment of the end of art coincides with that of the hegemony of the concept. We should connect this problematic back with the one we are immersed in nowadays, generalized logocentrism, and show that the art-industry belongs indirectly to this way of finishing art off. The art-industry would be a completion of speculative metaphysics, a way in which Hegel is present, has succeeded, in Hollywood. To be elucidated through Paul Virilio's remarks on the problem of space and time which he calls *critical*, in a strategic sense: that of the Pentagon. The position of Husserl in the face of the crisis of the sciences in Europe should also be elaborated.

A study of the advant-gardes is imperative. Their movement is not only due to the end of art. If they are in a problematic analogous to the one through which Hegel thematizes the end of art, they have 'exploited' this 'there remains only' in an exemplary way. If there remain only the conditions of space and time, in other words, basically, if representation, the staging of plots, are not interesting and what is interesting is Oedipus without a fate, then let's elaborate a painting of the fate-less. The avant-gardes get to work on the conditions of space and time. Attempts which have been going on for a century without having finished yet. This problematic makes it possible to resituate the real issue of the avant-gardes by putting them back in their domain. They have been inflexible witnesses to the crisis of these foundations of which theories of communication and the new technologies are other aspects, much less lucid ones than the avant-gardes. They at least had the sense of drama, and in this they are completely analogous in their own field to what has happened in the sciences.

115

From the end of the nineteenth century, there has been an immense amount of discussion under the heading of 'crisis of the sciences' – bearing on arithmetic, in other words the science of number which is the science of time; on geometry, the science of space; and on mechanics, the science of movement, which is to say the science of space and time. It is very hard to believe that what has been being discussed between scientists and philosophers for a century must be of no interest to the little ideology of communication. The problems out of which emerged non-Euclidean geometry, axiomatic forms of arithmetic and non-Newtonian physics are also those which gave rise to the theories of communication and information.

Is it the case that in this crisis, which bears on the conditions of space and time (with its two expressions: modern – there no longer remains anything but space and time; and postmodern – we no longer *even* have space and time left) – is it the case that in this work, which we take up under the aspect of communication, there is simply the loss of something (donation or presentation) without there being some gain? We are losing the earth (Husserl), which is to say the here-and-now, but are we gaining something and how are we gaining it? Can the uprooting which is linked to the new technology promise us an emancipation?

As is indicated in the conference's programme, the question of the body comes up here; but we must not put too much trust in this word, for if space and time are hit and attacked by the new technologies, then the body is too and has to be. Perhaps we should also set ourselves to the work of mourning the body.

About the confusion between passible and passive. These two problems are distinct: passivity is opposed to activity, but not passibility. Even further, this active/passive opposition presupposes passibility and at any rate is not what matters in the reception of works of art. The demand for an activity or 'interactivity' instead proves that there should be more intervention, and that we are thus through with aesthetic feeling. When you painted, you did not ask for 'interventions' from the one who looked, you claimed there was a community. The aim nowadays is not that sentimentality you still

116

find in the slightest sketch by a Cézanne or a Degas, it is rather that the one who receives should not receive, it is that s/he does not let him/herself be put out, it is his/her self-constitution as active subject in relation to what is addressed to him/her: let him/her reconstitute himself immediately and identify himself or herself as someone who intervenes. What we live by and judge by is exactly this will to action. If a computer invites us to play or *lets* us play, the interest valorized is that the one receiving should manifest his or her capacity for initiative, activity, etc. We are thus still derivatives from the Cartesian model of 'making oneself master and possessor . . .'. It implies the retreat of the passibility by which alone we are fit to receive and, as a result, to modify and do, and perhaps even to enjoy. This passibility as *jouissance* and obligatory belonging to an immediate community is repressed nowadays in the general problematic of communication, and is even taken as shameful. But to take action in the direction of this activity which is so sought-after is only to *react*, to repeat, at best to conform feverishly to a game that is already given or installed [*gestellt?*]. Passibility, in contrast, has to do with an immediate community of feeling demanded across the singular aesthetic feeling, and what is lost is more than simple capacity, it is propriety. Interactional ideology is certainly opposed to a passivity but it remains confined in a completely secondary opposition.

The true issue is to know whether or not are maintained the actuality and immediacy of a feeling which appeals to the co-belonging to a 'ground' presupposed by concept and calculation in their eluding of it. The work is only first *received* in the name of this immediate community, even if afterwards it can be presented in a gallery, at a distance. We are dealing with a problem of the modality of presence and not a problem of content or simple form. The question of unanimity of feeling bears not on what is presented or on the forms of presentation, but on the modality of reception, as demand for unanimity. It is not a matter of situating passibility as a moment, even a brief one, in a process of appropriation of the work, it is a matter of saying (and this is what is meant by *transcendental critique* in Kant) that without this dimension, we are incapable of so much as recognizing a

117

SOMETHING LIKE: 'COMMUNICATION . . . WITHOUT COMMUNICATION'

work *of art*. It is an a priori condition even if it is never marked in a perceptible way in the psycho-social process.

What is absolutely specific in art? What do space and time have to do with it? What is the gain from techno-science? What will become of our body? It is not in the discourse of techno-science, which *de facto* and *de jure* takes place outside this situation, but in the quite different field of the will to identification, that we will be able so much as to broach these questions.

Passibility: the opposite of 'impassibility'? Something is not destined for you, there is no way to feel it. You are touched, you will only *know* this afterwards. (And in thinking you know it, you will be mistaken about this 'touch'.) We imagine that minds are made anxious by not intervening in the production of the product. It is because we think of presence according to the exclusive modality of masterful intervention. Not to be contemplative is a sort of implicit commandment, contemplation is perceived as a devalorized passivity.

In Kant, passibility does not diappear with the sublime but becomes a passibility *to lack*. It is precisely the beautiful forms with their destination, our own destiny, which are missing, and the sublime includes this sort of pain due to the finitude of 'flesh', this ontological melancholy.

The question raised by the new technologies in connection with their relation to art is that of the here-and-now. What does 'here' mean on the phone, on television, at the receiver of an electronic telescope? And the 'now'? Does not the 'tele-' element necessarily destroy presence, the 'here-and-now' of the forms and their 'carnal' reception? What is a place, a moment, not anchored in the immediate 'passion' of what happens? Is a computer in any way here and now? Can anything *happen* with it? Can anything happen *to* it?

9

Representation, Presentation, Unpresentable

PAINTING AND POLITICAL REPRESENTATION

It is not only photography that made the craft of painting 'impossible'. That would be like saying that the work of Mallarmé or Joyce was a riposte to the progress of journalism. The 'impossibility' comes from the techno-scientific world of industrial and post-industrial capitalism. This world needs photography, but has almost no need for painting, just as it needs journalism more than literature. But above all it is possible only with the retreat of 'noble' crafts which belong to another world, and in the retreat of that world itself.

Painting obtained its letters of nobility, was placed among the fine arts, was given almost princely rights, during the Quattrocentro. Since then and for centuries, it made its contribution to the fulfilment of the metaphysical and political programme for the organization of the visual and the social. Optical geometry, the ordering of values and colours in line with a Neoplatonically inspired hierarchism, the rules for fixing the high points of religious or historical legend, helped to encourage the identification of new political communities: the city, the State, the nation, by giving them the destiny of seeing everything and of making the world transparent (clear and distinct) to monocular vision. Once placed on the perspectivist stage, the various components of the communities – narrative, urbanistic, architectural, religious, ethical – were put in order under the eye of the painter, thanks to the *costruzione legittima*. And in turn the eye of the monarch, positioned as indicated by the vanishing-point, receives this universe thus placed in order. When they are exhibited in the palace rooms of the lords or the people, and in churches, these representations offer all the members of the community the same possibility of identifying their belonging to this universe, as though they were the monarch or the painter. The modern notion of culture is born in the public access to the signs of historico-political identity and their collective deciphering. The Republic is heralded in this 'as-if-Prince', museums perpetuate this function, but reciprocally a glance at the House or the Senate in Washington, at the *Chambre des députés* in Paris, attests to the fact that this organization of space is not confined to pictures in a museum, but that it structures the representation of the political body itself. One sees in such places to what extent the Greek and Roman disposition of public spaces serves as a paradigm of socio-political space – even if as a phantasy – in the same way as in classical painting.

Photography brings to its end the programme of metapolitical ordering of the visual and the social. It finishes it in both senses of the word: it accomplishes it, and it puts an end to it. Know-how and knowledge as worked out, used and transmitted through studios and schools, are objectified in the camera. One click, and the most modest citizen, as amateur or tourist, produces his picture, organizes his space of identification, enriches his cultural memory, shares his prospectings. The perfecting of today's cameras liberates the user from worries about the exposure time, about focus, about aperture, about development. Tasks whose acquisition by the apprentice painter in the studio demanded huge experience (destroy bad habits, instruct the eye, the hand, the body, the mind, raise them to a new height) are programmed into the camera thanks to its refined optical, chemical, mechanical and electronic abilities. The amateur still has the choice of settings and subject. There too, he is guided by habits and connotations, but he can get free of them and seek out the unknown. Which he does. Rather than a tiresome recognition-process, amateur photography has become over the decades an instrument for prospecting and discovering, almost for ethnological enquiry. The old political function splits up, the ethnologist is a painter of little ethnic groups, the community has less need to identify with its prince, its centre, than to explore its edges. Amateur photographers have light-weight experiences and bring back documents.

Painters had already got down to the work of documentation (think of Courbet and Manet), but are rapidly defeated. Their procedures are not competitive: too slow in terms of professional training, too costly in materials, too long in the making, difficult upkeep of object, in short, expense of the whole process, compared with the tiny global cost of a photo. With the photo, the industrial *ready-made* wins out. Duchamp concludes that the time for painting has gone. Those who persist have to take on the challenge of photography. They move into the dialectic of the avant-gardes. What is at stake in this dialectic is the question, 'What is painting?', and what keeps the dialectic moving is the refutation of what was done or has just been done: no, *that* wasn't indispensable to painting either. Painting thus becomes a philosophical activity: the rules of formation of pictural images are not already stated and awaiting application. Rather, painting has as its rule to seek out these rules of formation of pictural images, as philosophy has as its rule to seek out the rules of philosophical sentences.

The avant-gardes thus cut themselves off from the public. The public brandishes cameras and flicks through 'clean' illustrations (at the cinema too). It is convinced that the programme of artificial perspective must be completed and does not understand how one can spend a year painting a white square, i.e. in representing nothing (unless it be that there is some unpresentable).

PHOTOGRAPHY AND INDUSTRIAL TECHNO-SCIENCE

Photography thus occupied the field opened by the classical aesthetics of images, the aesthetics of the beautiful. Like classical painting, it appeals to a taste: a sort of common sense ought in principle to come to an agreement on the disinterested pleasure given by an image faced with which the sensibility to forms and colours on the one hand, and the faculty of rational organization (the understanding) on the other, find themselves in free harmony. And yet the nature of this accord is profoundly modified in photography as it is in the whole field of aesthetic objects in the world of capitalist techno-science. Kant insisted on the fact that the accord must remain free – i.e. that it is not ruled a priori by laws. The massive introduction of industrial and post-industrial techno-sciences, of which photography is only one aspect, obviously implies the meticulous programming, through optical, chemical and photo-electronic means, of the fabrication of beautiful images. The indeterminate, because it cannot be forecast, has to be, if not eliminated, at least limited to the capacities of the apparatus, and with it sentiment too. Of course the artist, as always, plays with these constraints. But the common addressee of beautiful photos is not a sensory subject inventing a community of taste to come, but the addressee of finite products in which he must recognize the perfection of the procedures determining them. Industrial photography does not appeal to the beauty of sentiment, but to the beauty of understanding or connotation. It has the infallibility of what is perfectly programmed, the beauty of Voyager II.

The loss of *aura* is the negative aspect of this hardness, of the *hardware* implied in the fabrication of the apparatus that produces the photo. The amateur retains the choice of subject and settings, but the manner is that of the maker of the apparatus, in other words a state of industrial techno-science. Experience is that mass of affects, projects and memories that must perish and be born for a subject to arrive at the expression of what it is. As work, photography has almost nothing to do with this experience. It owes almost everything to the experimentation of industrial research laboratories. As a result, it is not beautiful, but *too beautiful*. And yet something is indicated by this *too*, an infinite, which is not the indeterminacy of a sentiment but the infinite realization of the sciences, technologies and capitalism. The definition of realities is indefinitely referred by the recurrence of analyses and the invention of axiomatics; the performativity of the instruments is in principle subject to obsolescence because of the incessant effects of fundamental research into technologies; the realization of capitalist surplus-value demands the perpetual reformulation of commodities and the opening of new markets. The hardness of industrial beauty contains within it the infinite of techno-scientific and economic reasons.

The destruction of experience, of which this is the sign, is not due simply to the entry of the 'well thought out' into the aesthetic field. To say only that would be to accept a positivist epistemology and sociology. Science, technology and capital, even in their matter–of–fact style, are so many ways of actualizing the infinity of concepts. Knowing everything, being able to do everything, having everything are horizons, and horizons are at an infinite distance. It is this infinite which paradoxically presents itself ready–made in established knowledge, in the apparatuses and weapons currently in use, in invested capital and commodities and in photographs. It presents itself as what, in objects, finishes them, i.e. gives them their perfection and announces their destruction.

This is why amateur photography, which at first sight is not much more than the consumption of the capacity for images contained in the camera, is also, in the infinite dialectic of concepts being realized, the consumption of a state of objects and of knowledge; and why it already calls for a new state of those objects and that knowledge. The amateur is in this way in the service of experimentation carried out by laboratories and ordered by banks. The end of experience is doubtless the end of the subjective infinite, but, as a negative moment in the dialectics of research, it is the concretization of an anonymous infinite that ceaselessly organizes and disorganizes the world, and of which the individual subject, at whatever level she be in the social hierarchy, is the voluntary or involuntary servant.

It follows that the definition of what is a good photographic image, which was initially linked to the rules of artificial perspective, is subject to revision. Photography too enters the field opened by infinite research. Its initial function, inherited from the task of identification assigned to painting by the Quattrocentro, falls out of use as the major concern for the community's self-identification falls out of use. In the current state of techno-science and capital, the identification of the community with itself has no need of the support of minds, it does not require any shared great ideologies, but takes place through the mediation of the whole set of goods and services exchanged at a prodigious speed, of the general equivalent of the exchanges, i.e. money, and the absolute presupposed of this equivalent, i.e. language. And so research for knowledge, technologies and investments on the verge of the twenty-first century bears on languages. The traditional function of the political institution undergoes a displacement: its purpose is less to embody the Idea of the community, and it is more turned towards the management of infinite research for knowledge, know-how and wealth. In this general movement, photography is released from the responsibilities of ideological identification it had inherited from the tradition of painting, and it henceforth gives rise to research. Photographic art appears, and it is exercised jointly by professional researchers and by artists, as is the case in the other industrial arts. We are no longer at the stage of deploring the 'mechanical reproduction' of works; we know that industry does not mean the end of the arts, but their mutation. The question 'What is photography?' draws these attempts into a dialectic comparable with that of the avant-gardes in painting – I mean a negative dialectic.

WHAT IS AT STAKE IN THE AVANT-GARDES IN PAINTING?

The avant-gardes, facing the inanity ('chocolate-box', 'official art') of the craft of painting in a community without prince or people, turn to the question, 'What is painting?' One after another, the presuppositions implied by the exercise of the craft are subjected to trial and contestation: local colour, linear perspective, the rendering of colour values, the frame, formats, hiding the support by covering the surface completely, the medium, the instrument, the place of exhibition, and many others beside, are plastically questioned by the various avant-gardes. 'Modern painters' discover that they have to form images that photography cannot present because those same presuppositions that their research interrogates and discovers are those that rule over the manufacture of cameras and because, in the photographic industry, they are what defines the ideal result, the 'good photo'. These painters discover that they have to present that there is something that is not presentable according to the legitimate construction. They begin to overturn the supposed 'givens' of the visible so as to make visible the fact that the visual field hides and requires invisibilities, that it does not simply belong to the eye (of the prince) but to the (wandering) mind.

They thus make painting enter the field opened by the aesthetics of the sublime. This aesthetics is not regulated by taste. That taste is a disinterested pleasure which in principle can be shared, and which proceeds from the free accord between the faculty of conceiving an 'object' and that of presenting in the sensible field an example of that 'object'. Avant-garde painting escapes *ex hypothesi* from the aesthetics of the beautiful, its works do not call for the 'common sense' of a shared pleasure. These works appear to the public of taste to be 'monsters', 'formless' objects, purely 'negative' entities (I'm deliberately using the terms Kant employs to character-ize the occasions that provoke the sublime sentiment). When the point is to try to present that there is something that is not presentable, you have to make presentation suffer. This means among other things that painters and public do not have at their disposal established symbols, figures or plastic forms which would allow them to signify and understand that the point of the work is Ideas of reason or imagination, as was the case in Romanesque Christian painting. In the techno-scientific industrial world, there can be no stable symbols of the good, the just, the true, the infinite, etc. Certain 'realisms' (which in fact are academicisms: bourgeois at the end of the nineteenth Century, socialist and national-socialist during the twentieth) attempt to reconstitute symbolic systems, to offer the public work it can enjoy and on the occasion of which it can identify with Images (race, socialism, nation, etc.). We know that this effort always demanded the elimination of the avant-gardes. The avant-gardes carry out a secret questioning of the 'technical' presuppositions of painting, which leads

125

them to a complete neglect of the 'cultural' function of stabilization of taste and identification of a community by means of visible symbols. An avant-garde painter feels first of all responsible to the demand coming from his activity itself, i.e. 'What is painting?'. And what is essentially at stake in his work is to show that there is invisibility in the visual. The task of 'cultivating' the public comes later.

The unpresentable is what is the object of an Idea, and for which one cannot show (present) an example, a case, even a symbol. The universe is unpresentable, so is humanity, the end of history, the instant, space, the good, etc. The absolute in general, says Kant. For to present is to relativize, to place into contexts and conditions of presentation, in this case plastic contexts and conditions. So one cannot present the absolute. But one can present that there is some absolute. This is a 'negative' (Kant also says 'abstract') presentation. The current of 'abstract' painting has its source, from 1912, in this requirement for indirect and all but ungraspable allusion to the invisible in the visible. The sublime, and not the beautiful, is the sentiment called forth by these works.

The sublime is not a pleasure, it is a pleasure of pain: we fail to present the absolute, and that is a displeasure, but we know that we have to present it, that the faculty of feeling or imagining is called on to bring about the sensible (the image). To present what reason can conceive, and even if it cannot manage to do this, and we suffer from this, a pure pleasure is felt from this tension. There is nothing surprising about finding the term 'sublime' in Apollinaire's studies on the *peintres artistes*, or in the titles and writings of Barnett Newman, or in texts published by several avant-gardist currents in the sixties and seventies. Obviously the word is from a romantic vocabulary.

The avant-gardes in painting fulfil romanticism, i.e. modernity, which, in its strong and recurrent sense, is the failure of stable regulation between the sensible and the intelligible. But at the same time they are a way out of romantic nostalgia because they do not try to find the unpresentable at a great distance, as a lost origin or end, to be represented in the subject of the picture, but in what is closest, in the very matter of artistic work. Baudelaire is still romantic, but Joyce

126

not very, and Gertrude Stein even less. Füssli or Caspar David Friedrich are romantic, as is Delacroix, Cézanne less so, Delaunay or Mondrian hardly at all. The last-named obey the experimenting vocation (in what they do, if not always in what they write), but especially the evocation of the unpresentable. Their sublime is scarcely a nostalgic one, being turned towards the infinity of plastic essays to be made rather than towards the representation of a supposedly lost absolute. Their work is thus in accord with the contemporary world of industrial techno-sciences at the same time as it disavows it.

As for the 'trans-avantgardism' of Bonito Oliva and the similar currents one can observe in the USA and Germany (including Jencks's 'postmodernism' in architecture, which the reader will do me the favour of not confusing with what I have called 'the postmodern condition'), it is clear that behind the pretext of picking up the tradition of the avant-gardes, this is a pretext for squandering it. This inheritance can only be transmitted in the negative dialectic of refutations and supplementary questionings. To want to get a result from it, especially by addition, is to arrest this dialectic, to confine the spirit of avant-gardist works to the museum, to encourage the eclecticism of consumption. Mixing on the same surface neo-. or hyper-realist motifs and abstract, lyrical or conceptual motifs means that everything is equivalent because everything is good for consumption. This is an attempt to establish and have approved a new 'taste'. This taste is no taste. What is called on by eclecticism are the habits of magazine readers, the needs of the consumer of standard industrial images – this is the spirit of the super-market shopper. To the extent that this postmodernism, via critics, museum and gallery directors and collectors, puts strong pressure on the artists, it consists in aligning research in painting with a *de facto* state of 'culture' and in deresponsibilizing the artists with respect to the question of the unpresentable. Now in my view this question is the only one worthy of what is at stake in life and thought in the coming century. Having this question forgotten is a threat which must not be neglected because it promises a loosening of the tension between the act of painting and the essence of painting, whereas this tension has persistently motivated one

127

of the most admirable centuries of Western painting. It brings with it the corruption of the honour of painting, which has remained intact in spite of the worst demands of States (make it cultural!) and the market (make money!).

The post-industrial techno-scientific world does not have as a general principle that one must present something that is not presentable, and thus represent it, but obeys the contrary principle, namely that the infinite is in play in the very dialectic of research. It is absurd, impracticable and reactionary to turn aside from this principle. What has to be done is to slip into it the evocation of the absolute. It is not the artist's job to restore a supposed 'reality' that the search for knowledge, techniques and wealth never stops destroying, only to reconstruct a version thought for a while to be more credible, and which will have to be abandoned in its turn. The spirit of the times is definitely not geared to what is pleasing, and the task of art remains that of the immanent sublime, that of alluding to an unpresentable which has nothing edifying about it, but which is inscribed in the infinity of the transformation of 'realities'. We know that this does not happen without anguish. But painters are not responsible to the question, 'How can we escape anguish?' They are responsible to the question, 'What is it to paint?' The fact that, as members of the 'intellectual class', they are also responsible to the question, 'How can we make those who are not artists understand our painting?', does not mean that the two responsibilities are to be confused.

That would be as though the philosopher confused his/her responsibility to thought with his/her responsiblity to the public. The question of how to make others understand what thinking is is the question of the intellectual. The philosopher asks only: 'What is thinking?' The public is not necessarily the interlocutor on this question. In fact, this question places philosophers too, today, in the position of an unknown avant-garde. That's why they dare talk about painters, their brothers or sisters in writing.

10

Speech Snapshot

– Do these women have souls? What do they want?

– Ask them.

– But to ask someone a question is to presuppose that that person understands it and wants to reply, that he wants to help you to know something, that he wants to know with you, co-operate in a dialogue, and therefore that he has a soul and wishes for the good. If they heard our question, we wouldn't have to ask ourselves whether they have souls and what they want, they would 'tell' us this clearly enough by hearing us. Do we ask ourselves this question about ourselves? The question as to whether they have a soul cannot be asked them without aporia: can you be the addressee of a question bearing on your ability to be the addressee of a question? And what is the soul and what is the will if not this possibility of being questioned?

– And yet the simplest way of finding out is to ask them. Either they will reply, and that will prove, whatever the reply, that they can indeed be questioned, that they want the good and have a soul. Or else they will not reply, and the question will remain your business, and you'll have to deal with it without them.

– They have not replied, you know that. They grimace, twist themselves about, tetanize themselves, crucify themselves, get ecstatic, hallucinate, catatonize and atonize, stifle, offer themselves and run away, in a debate of the body with something or someone we know not what and which, I assure you, is not us. Whence the problem, and the reason why we cannot accept the simple choice you suggest. For even if they don't hear us, it is still true that all this must have some sort of sense and in a certain way they must be 'replying' to us. It remains to find in what language and to whom. Now that cannot be done entirely without them. We argue about them, but they must still, even if involuntarily, offer us the documents and testimony which will serve as evidence for our argument. As to talking *about* them, failing the possibility of talking *with* them – so be it, we settle for that, since in any case we must speak and, if possible, say everything; but they will contribute, willy nilly, to the advancement of our research, we'll tear our evidence from them. We need signs.

– So this is what you imagine: perhaps they have a soul, perhaps they hear the question; but it is not your question, and you do not hear their reply; in principle you admit that the cries, contractions, fits and hallucinations observed during the attacks are, in some sense, replies; so you give yourself three things to construct – the language they speak with their bodies, the question to which their 'attacks' respond and the nature of what is questioning them.

– That's it, it's a problem of communication, i.e. translation. No doubt they do have a soul, but of a type different from ours, speak a language, but a bodily language (even their words are like things), they hear someone, but not us. We have to establish what they want. We record them every which way, like extraterrestrial beings. We describe their gesticulations exactly. And, you'll see, we shall decipher their idiom, they'll end up by talking to us. They will want to know,

130

like we do. They will enter our community. There will be no more hysterics.

– You mean that this strange, foreign idiom will be absorbed, that a universal language will permit the circulation and exchange of all meanings, you'll have finished with obscenity?

– Don't skimp on our trial like that. We shall leave them the singularity of their dialect. But we still have to show that the stuttering, the atrophies, the catatonias, all that vital dementia, are saying something, replying to some question. We have to show that they hear. Which we do by hypnotizing them, by making them do what we suggest. That proves their receptiveness to language.

– That's a language of prescriptions, not questions ... You give them instructions like automata, but these are heteromata because their soul is outside them. To carry out an order is not to reply to a question.

– Granted. But the path ahead is traced out. It will suffice for you to imagine this: the concatenation of postures constituting the mime of the attack follows a scenario. This scenario is what is dictated to them, they play it. So they hear instructions, and carry them out on their bodies.

– That's still talking about an automaton, you're not getting close to their soul. Or else, have the courage to recognize that this carrying out is an interpretation like in the theatre or the cinema and presupposes not only that the orders are heard, but a subtle listening to what the scenario demands. Have the courage to say that their soul inhabits their body, but that that is only possible if the body has soul. That they have what is called a talent for expression. That you and I do not have this talent, relegating this type of expressive essay to the ephemeral, confused and unobservable stage of dreams, where it is quickly forgotten. Whereas they bear them superbly on

131

the stage of their visible flesh (which gives you the opportunity of photographing them), indifferent as they are, like the great artists, to whomever will be the addressee of these ecstatic snapshots, playing for an audience which is not that of your assistants, my dear Doctor, nor that of your students, nor that of the technicians, nor even for you and your photograhers ignoring as simply mistakes the suspect interest of the ward-boy and the meticulous curiosity of the big boss, seeking to invent, between what's common in the former and what's distinguished in the latter, another genre which would be no more comic than tragic.

We lookers, exempt from the work of the hospital ward, the lecture-hall and the consulting-room, we examine the collection of these photographs in a review, a century later. The women whose photos we see are not ill, in the process of betraying or exhibiting their symptoms. They are not savages, prey to the trances of divination or exorcism. They are not even actresses caught live at the high-point of their performance.

They teach us a sort of theatre of corporeal elements: the pupil, through dilation; the naso-labial fold through contraction; the wrist through blocking in orthogonal position of the forearm, the network of muscles of the posterior through fixing in an arc on nape and heels. It can be through collapsing, in lethargies, or through optimal condition, in ecstasy, that the element is designated.

They were photographed to make up an album of hysteria, so as to decipher what they might possibly be saying by these postures. Which implies this: that these bodily states were semantic elements and that they could be linked together by a syntax. One would thus obtain sentences, regulated sequences, and, along with them, meaning. But the photograph which was to make them speak produces an opposite impression on us. It fixes the states in their suspended instability, isolates them one from another, does

132

not restore the syntax linking them. It makes us see
tensorial stances.

These have a relation to the bodily syntax (of traditional
theatre or dance) like that of little elements of sound to
composed music. John Cage says that he wants to let
sounds be. These photos show what it is to let body-states
be.

They illustrate almost perfectly what Richard Foreman asks
of the ontological-hysterical theatre: 'Make everything
dumb enough to allow what is happening to happen.'* And
when Foreman declares that

> Most art is
> created by
> people trying to
> make their idea,
> emotion, thing-
> imagined, *be-there*
> *more*. They re-
> inforce. I want
> my imagined to be an
> occasion wherein the not-imagined-by-me can be
> there†

it is as though we were hearing today what Charcot's
patients want.

They are those 'characters' (Foreman's quotes: MY
'characters') whose 'task' is to identify with a consciousness

> which . . . doesn't SUSTAIN objects in the mind . . .
> but presents and represents
> in every tiny quanta of time
> the content.‡

*Richard Foreman, 'Ontological-hysteric: Manifesto I', in *Plays and
Manifestos*, ed. Kate Davy (New York: New York University Press,
1976), p. 77.
†Ibid., p. 76.
‡Ibid., p. 138.

These photos are representations of quantic presentations of tonic content.

– Do you think you are going to save these sick women by making works of art, or artists, out of them? (And at the cost of what torture inflicted on art?)

– They insist. They want these women to say something, a primal scene, a hypnosis, a fantasm, the castration of those who observe them, impossible love, playing at being a man. But if they have a soul, it is not in proposing a discourse open to discussion, even one that's a bit askew, but in murmuring-shouting with Rhoda:
Oh I'm as clear as a muscle. Oh Eleanor PAINT me.*

The photo ceases to support the argumentation of the scientists, it suspends the dialectic (for an instant), unleashed tableau vivant. Grasp me if you can. But it will be or has been too early or too late. Is an accent (an accent in the state of the body) graspable outside of succession? Hysteria would not only be an illness, rather an ontological essay on time. Or, better: the former by virtue of the latter. Photography reveals this because it is a hysteria of the gaze just as much as a means of control.

*Richard Foreman, 'Pain(t)', ibid., p. 205

11

After the Sublime, the State of Aesthetics

I should like to focus the examination of this 'state' on the question of matter. I shall give only a rapid sketch of the argument.

(1) It seems to me indispensable to go back through the Analytic of the Sublime from Kant's *Critique of Judgement* in order to get an idea of what is at stake in modernism, in what are called the avant-gardes in painting or in music. I take from it the following principles:

For the last century, the arts have not had the beautiful as their main concern, but something which has to do with the sublime. I am not including those recent currents that are bringing painting, architecture or music back round to the traditional values of taste – I mean trans-avantgardism, neo-expressionism, the new subjectivity, postmodernism, etc.: the neo-'s and the post-'s. I put these down to an overlapping of two orders of activity that it is necessary to keep apart from each other: the order of cultural activities and that of artistic work. Each of these obeys specific laws. Painters or writers (or musicians, etc.) have to reply to the question: 'What is it to write?', 'What is it to paint?' On the other hand, they can be the object of a demand coming from a real or virtual audience, audible these days on the cultural market and through the culture-industry. It is not, for example, the same thing to have to think and to have to teach. Teaching is (or has become) a cultural activity, at least to the extent that it is subordinated to a demand coming from a community. I have no contempt for cultural activities. they too can and should be properly carried out. Simply, they are quite different from what I'm here calling artistic work (including thought).

(2) One of the essential features revealed by Kant's analysis of the sublime depends on the disaster suffered by the imagination in the sublime sentiment. In Kant's architectonic of the faculties, the imagination is the power or the faculty of presentation. Of presenting not only *sensoria*, but also, when the imagination works *freely* (without bending to the conditions required by the understanding, by the faculty of concepts), with a view to establishing a knowledge of experience. In its very freedom, the imagination is the faculty of presenting *data* in general, including 'imaginative' or even 'created' *data*, as Kant calls them.

As every presentation consists in the 'forming' of the matter of the data, the disaster suffered by the imagination can be understood as the sign that the forms are not relevant to the sublime sentiment. But in that case, where does matter stand, if the forms are no longer there to make it *presentable*? How is it with presence?

(3) With a view to resolving this paradox of an aesthetics without sensible or imaginative forms, Kant's thought looks towards the principle that an Idea of Reason is revealed at the same time as the imagination proves to be impotent in *forming* data. In the sublime 'situation', something like an Absolute, either of magnitude or of power, is made quasi-perceptible (the word is Kant's) due to the very failing of the faculty of presentation. This Absolute is, in Kant's terminology, the object of an Idea of Reason.

(4) We might wonder whether this slippage or returning of imagination to pure reason (theoretical or practical) leaves room for an aesthetic. The principal *interest* that Kant sees in the sublime sentiment is that it is the 'aesthetic' (negative) sign of a transcendence proper to ethics, the transcendence of the moral law and of freedom. In any case, the sublime

cannot be the fact of a human art, or even of a nature 'complicit' (through its 'cipher writing', the beautiful forms it proposes to the mind) with our sentiment. On the contrary, in the sublime, nature stops addressing itself to us in this language of forms, in these visual or sound 'landscapes' which bring about the pure pleasure of the beautiful and inspire commentary as an attempt at decipherment. Nature is no longer the sender of secret sensible messages of which the imagination is the addressee. Nature is 'used', 'exploited' by the mind according to a purposiveness that is not nature's, not even the purposiveness without purpose implied in the pleasure of the beautiful.

Kant writes that the sublime is a *Geistesgefühl*, a sentiment of the mind, whereas the beautiful is a sentiment that proceeds from a 'fit' between nature and mind, i.e., when transcribed into the Kantian economy of faculties, between the imagination and the understanding. This marriage or, at least, this betrothal proper to the beautiful is broken by the sublime. The Idea, especially the Idea of pure practical reason, Law and freedom, is signalled in a quasi-perception right within the break-up of the imagination and therefore just as much via a lack or even a disappearance of nature understood in this way. The *Geistesgefühl*, the sentiment of the mind, signifies that the mind is lacking in nature, that nature is lacking for it. It feels only itself. In this way the sublime is none other than the sacrificial announcement of the ethical in the aesthetic field. Sacrificial in that it requires that imaginative nature (inside and outside the mind) must be sacrificed in the interests of practical reason (which is not without some specific problems for the *ethical* evaluation of the sublime sentiment). This heralds the end of an aesthetics, that of the beautiful, in the name of the final destination of the mind, which is freedom.

(5) On the basis of these rapid considerations, the question is this: what is an *art*, painting or music, an art and not a moral practice, in the context of such a disaster? What can an art be that must operate not only without a determinant concept (as shown by the Analytic of the Beautiful), but also without a spontaneous form, without a free form, as is the case in taste?

What is still in play for the mind when it is dealing with presentation (which is the case with every art), when presentation itself seems impossible?

(6) We have, I believe, an advantage over Kant (it's only a matter of chronology) in that we have at our disposal the experiments and essays of Western painters and musicians of the last 200 years. It would be arrogant and stupid to claim to assign only one meaning to the superabundant spread of their achievement in this period. But I would like to pick out one point which to me seems highly relevant and enlightening within the hypothesis of the formless, inherited from Kant's analysis. This point concerns matter, by which I mean matter in the arts, i.e. presence.

(7) It has been a presupposition, or even a prejudice, a ready-made attitude, in Western thought at least, for 2,000 years, that the process of art is to be understood as a relating of a matter and a form. This prejudice is still active even in Kant's analysis. What guarantees the purity of taste, what withdraws aesthetic pleasure from the action of empirical interests, 'pathological' preferences, the satisfaction of particular motivations is, according to Kant, the consideration of form alone, indifference to the quality or properly material power of the sensory or even imaginative data. If one likes a flower for its colour or a sound for its timbre, this is like preferring one dish to another, a question of idiosyncrasy. This type of empirical pleasure cannot hope to be universally shared. If on the contrary a given singular taste is to be that of anyone and everyone, as is demanded by the pleasure brought about by beauty, this promise can only be grounded on the form of the object procuring that pleasure. This is because form represents a case, the simplest and perhaps most fundamental case, of what for Kant constitutes the property common to every mind: its capacity (power, faculty) to synthesize data, gather up the manifold, the *Mannigfaltigkeit* in general. And the *matter* of data is represented as what is *par excellence* diverse, unstable and evanescent.

That is the basis for an Aesthetics of the Beautiful. What is called formalism is to all appearances the final attempt accomplished within the framework of this aesthetics, but one which elaborates the very conditions of presentation.

(8) *Mutatis mutandis*, we would find this same opposition and hierarchy in the Aristotelian theme of nature as art and art as nature. Matter is put on the side of power, but of power conceived of as potential, as an indeterminate state of reality, whereas form, with its own mode of causality, is thought of as the act giving a figure to material power. There is in this a sort of 'fit' which has to be seen as a correspondence between an obscure and vague push (a push, a growth, *phusis* as the power of the *phuein*, to grow), the push that is the business of matter, on the one hand, and on the other a specific and determining call coming from the final form for which the material power is waiting. This vast metaphysical set-up is placed under the regime of the principle of purposiveness.

(9) As the idea of a natural fit between matter and form declines (a decline already implied in Kant's analysis of the sublime (and one that for a century was both hidden and shown up by the aesthetics of romanticism), the aim for the arts, especially of painting and music, can only be that of approaching matter. Which means approaching presence without recourse to the means of presentation. We can manage to determine a colour or a sound in terms of vibrations, by specifying pitch, duration and frequency. But timbre and nuance (and both terms apply to the quality of colours as well as to sonorities) are precisely what escape this sort of determination.

The same goes for forms. In general, the value of a colour is considered to depend on the place it occupies among others on the surface of the picture, and to be thus dependent on the form of that picture. This is what's called the problem of composition, and is therefore a matter of comparison. It is hard to grasp a nuance in itself. And yet, if we suspend the activity of comparing and grasping, the aggressivity, the 'hands-on' [*mancipium*] and the negotiation that are the regime of mind, then, through this ascesis (Adorno), it is perhaps not impossible to become open to the invasion of nuances, passible to timbre.

Nuance and timbre are scarcely perceptible differences between sounds or colours which are otherwise identical in terms of the determination of their physical parameters. This difference can be due, for example, to the way they are obtained: for example, the same note coming from a violin, a piano or a flute, the same colour in pastel, oil or watercolour. Nuance and timbre are what *differ* and *defer*, what makes the difference between the note on the piano and the same note on the flute, and thus what also defer the identification of that note.

Within the tiny space occupied by a note or a colour in the sound- or colour-continuum, which corresponds to the identity-card for the note or the colour, timbre or nuance introduce a sort of infinity, the indeterminacy of the harmonics within the frame determined by this identity. Nuance or timbre are the distress and despair of the exact division and thus the clear composition of sounds and colours according to graded scales and harmonic temperaments.

From this aspect of matter, one must say that it must be immaterial. Immaterial if it is envisaged under the regime of receptivity or intelligence. For forms and concepts are constitutive of objects, they pro-duce data that can be grasped by sensibility and that are intelligible to the understanding, things over there which fit the faculties or capacities of the mind. The matter I'm talking about is 'immaterial', an-objectable, because it can only 'take place' or find its occasion at the price of suspending these active powers of the mind. I'd say that it suspends them for at least 'an instant'. However, this instant in turn cannot be counted, since in order to count this time, even the time of an instant, the mind must be active. So we must suggest that there is a state of mind which is a prey to 'presence' (a presence which is in no way present in the sense of *here-and-now*, i.e. like what is designated by the deictics of presentation), a mindless state of mind, which is required of mind not for matter to be perceived or conceived, given or grasped, but *so that there be* some something. And I use 'matter' to designate this '*that there is*', this *quod*, because this presence in the absence of the active mind is and is never other than timbre, tone, nuance in one or other of the dispositions of sensibility, in one or other of the *sensoria*, in one or other of the possibilities through which mind is accessible to the material event, can be 'touched' by it: a singular, incomparable quality – unforgettable and immediately forgotten – of the grain of a skin or a piece of wood, the fragrance of an aroma, the savour of a secretion or a piece of flesh, as well as a timbre or a nuance. All these terms are interchangeable. They all designate the event of a passion, a possibility for which the mind will not have been prepared, which will have unsettled it, and of which it conserves only the feeling – anguish and jubilation – of an obscure debt.

(10) In one of his letters, Cézanne writes: 'Form is finished when colour reaches perfection.' What is going on here in the work of painting is not at all to cover [*color*, same root as *celare*, to conceal, to hide] the support by filling in a form drawn in advance with chromatic material. On the contrary, the point is to begin or try to begin by depositing a 'first' touch of colour, let another one come along, then another nuance, letting them associate through a demand which is their own and which has to be felt, where the thing is not to make oneself master of it. There is an analogous remark in a note by Matisse about a large piece called *Mémoire d'Océanie*, watercolour and collage on paper, which is in the Musuem of Modern Art in New York. It is clear too that from Debussy to Boulez, Cage or Nono, via Webern or Varèse, the attention of modern musicians has been turned towards this secret possibility to sound-timbre. And it is also this that makes jazz and electronic music important. For with gongs and in general all percussion instruments, with synthesizers, musicians have access to an infinite continuum of sound-nuances. And I think that we'd need to reconsider from this angle, that of immaterial matter, certain Minimalist or *arte povera* works, and certain works called abstract expressionist or not (I'm thinking of certain pieces from the Cobra group).

(11) This interest for matter involves a paradox. The matter thus invoked is something that is not finalized, not destined. It is in no way a material whose function would be to fill a form and actualize it. We have to say that, thought of in this

141

way, matter would be something which is not *addressed*, what does not *address* itself to the mind (what in no way enters into a pragmatics of communicational and teleological destination).

The paradox of art 'after the sublime' is that it turns towards a thing which does not turn towards the mind, that it wants a thing, or *has it in for* a thing which wants nothing of it. After the sublime, we find ourselves after the will. By matter, I mean *the Thing*. The Thing is not waiting to be destined, it is not waiting for anything, it does not call on the mind. How can the mind situate itself, get in touch with something that withdraws from every relationship?

It is the destiny or destination of the mind to question (as I have just done). And to question is to attempt to establish the relation of something with something. Matter does not question the mind, it has no need of it, it exists, or rather *insists*, it sists 'before' questioning and answer, 'outside' them. It is presence as unpresentable to the mind, always withdrawn from its grasp. It does not offer itself to dialogue and dialectic.

(12) Can we find an analogue of matter in the order of thought itself? Is there a matter of thought, a nuance, a grain, a timbre which makes an event for thought and unsettles it, analogously with what I have described in the sensory order? Perhaps here we have to invoke words. Perhaps words themselves, in the most secret place of thought, are its matter, its timbre, its nuance, i.e. what it cannot manage to think. Words 'say', sound, touch, always 'before' thought. And they always 'say' something other than what thought signifies, and what it wants to signify by putting them into form. Words want nothing. They are the 'un-will', the 'non-sense' of thought, its mass. They are innumerable like the nuances of a colour- or sound-continuum. They are always older than thought. They can be semiologized, philologized, just as nuances are chromatized and timbres gradualized. But like timbres and nuances, they are always being born. Thought tries to tidy them up, arrange them, control them and manipulate them. But as they are old people and children, words are not obedient. As Gertrude Stein thought, to write

142

is to respect their candour and their age, as Cézanne or Karel Appel respect colours.

(13) From this point of view, theory, aesthetic theory, seems, will have seemed to be the attempt by which the mind tries to rid itself of words, of the matter that they are, and finally of matter itself. Happily, this attempt has no chance of success. One cannot get rid of the Thing. Always forgotten, it is unforgettable.

12

Conservation and Colour

I shall speak only about the museum of painting. Of what is called painting. Or: *pigmenta* as *picta*. Colour, posed, disposed, proposed, exposed. And, in the museum, re-posed, or posed once for all times, already and still posed and to be posed. Conserved, we say. With this connotation from the Latin *servare*: to keep up [*entre-tenir*: literally, to hold between], to maintain, to remain and cause to remain. Conservation as an *entretien infini*.*

It's a strange obstination or destination, to maintain and entertain posed paint. It has a relationship to time. The posed paint will not 'pass', it will always be now. That's the principle.

One might think that this condition (more demand than situation), is common to every enterprise of conservation, that it is the presumption, not of any memory (which, as we know, overflows both broadly and insidiously – I mean from the outside, but from the inside too – the programme of intentions to remember), but one might think that this remained common at least to any voluntary, intentional memorization. Which cannot happen without the inscription of the thing to be maintained outside forgetting.

---

*Entretien has the sense both of 'conversation' or 'interview', and that of 'maintenance' and 'upkeep': the immediate allusion here is to Maurice Blanchot's book *L'entretien infini* (Paris: Gallimard, 1969), as referred to a little later. (Translators' note)

144

'Inscription' means that the thing can pass, cannot not pass, but that the signs which signal that it was then remain there. And when we say 'remain there', we presuppose, with that 'there', the salvation that every memorization expects from space. This is the very argument which supports the supposed 'refutation' of Idealism in Kant's first *Critique*. We presuppose that *servare*, that *salvare* of the inscription, or we imply it. Graphics, engraving makes a trace, whatever it may be, that the thing has been. The picture in the museum is of course no longer the 'picture itself', as one says the 'thing itself': so we think, so we all think, enemies *and* friends of the museum. It is the trace of its past presence, and it makes a sign, a mnesic sign in the direction of its supposed initial state, let's say of appearing.

The whole space of exhibition becomes the remains of a time; all the places, here, indices for other, past, times, the olden days; the look, now, of the looker, the visitor, on the paint makes it into the sign of the paint it was, in its position or pose at the beginning of the work, at the moment of the *opus*'s operation. And that can be said, so it seems, of any work, a house, a town, a landscape too, a book. The exhibition, says J.- L. Déotte, submerges every position. The worked space is a memorandum, the coloured space included.

You will remember that it is upon this presupposition or this implication, according to which space conserves, but conserves only by converting the thing into its sign, or by replacing it with its archive, that Plato's condemnation of writing in the *Phaedrus* rests. Graphics is a mnemotechnic. It transcribes for us what was said and thought then. It maintains and entertains the dialogue with self that is thought, it allows it to reach posterity, but it disarms it, blunts its living point. Writing delivers to readers, to their minds, a thought deprived of the faculty or rather of the actuality of that faculty to bounce back, to start again, to ask again, to accept the question raw, to make room for the void of what is not yet thought. Through inscription, tradition betrays what it conserves. The time of transmission is a dead time, that of a repetition of the same through moments not distinguished by the event. It is still this presupposition, scarcely displaced, that orders Bergson's opposition of spatialized time with living duration.

Many of the accusations levelled at the museum proceed from this presupposition. It is only, they say, a mnemotechnic device. The works exhibited in it are emptied, bloodless. They are no longer valid for themselves, in their presence, but as signs of a lost life, and again, and perhaps above all, as testimony to the power – very current and present – to conserve. The power of the curators. And finally, according to this logic, the museum exhibits itself as a work of conservation. A work of the conservation of works. The 'colour' of an art museum, its timbre, its tone, its own atmosphere exercise its hegemony over the colours posed and composed in the painted works. The first is obtained by a composition of the second. The artists pass over into subservience to the curators. Even here, in our workshop, the absence of artists, as Buren pointed out to me when he'd read our programme, testifies in favour of this necrosis. The dead grips the living.

It would be possible to think that this is 'merely', so to speak, a question of a change of frame, or scale, what Buren himself has been criticizing for fifteen years (I'm thinking of one of his first texts, *Critical Limits*, which dates from 1970). The museum of painting is itself a work of painting. But it is not a simple enlargement of the frame or the scale, it is also a decisive transformation of the destination of the work, at least in Buren's view. For the museum-work has as its end the conservation, upkeep [*entretien*] and maintenance, and therefore mnemotechnics alone. Whereas this is not true at all, at least if one follows Buren's initial hypothesis, of the painted work. It is living, one-off, i.e. situated and momentary. I'd say that in this approach it is essentially expenditure rather than reserve, and that if it is exhibited or exposed, it is rather to the uncertainty of its future than to its perpetual right to a place in the cultural heritage.

There is, or was, in Buren's polemic with conservation, a recurrence of the properly Platonic motif of the life of works. The term *entretien*, which is understood as *maintien*, maintaining, mnemotechnics, also means its opposite, a holding of meaning ceaselessly exposed to the event, to the question, to the taking up again, to the re-working of the maintenance of the theme, as in Blanchot's *L'entretien infini.*

And if we push a little in this direction, we will not be able to rest content with the principle of the so-called 'open' work, for it is the very notion of a work at all, as gathering and pose, for example of the painting as position and finished composition of colours, which needs to be questioned. In such a problematic, which rests, I repeat and stress, on the presupposition that the first gesture, *live*, 'presence', can only be damaged and pass or fade, as a colour fades when it is retained, reserved and conserved – and because of this very reserve – in this problematic, the institution of the museum seems as though it ought to be condemned without appeal. Simply because it is *par excellence* the finished work, the work in which works are finished.

If we want to confirm that this problematic, which is Platonic and entirely metaphysical, is still active and alive, it is enough to read the reflections inspired by photographic art (it keeps the thing alive by killing it), or to observe the media's penchant for 'live' transmission and recording (the words are revealing) on records: recording, i.e. what is deferred.

We philosophers have been in the habit of ignoring this prejudice for years now. Of doing the critique of the 'first draft', of the origin, of life, and this is also a critique of the act, of pure actuality, and of the now . . . . By showing that one is always and everywhere dealing with differing/deferring. This critique is called 'grammatology' when it emphasizes that nothing is that is not inscribed, 'written' in the sense Derrida gives to this term. Or, following Deleuze's path, that there is no difference that does not presuppose repetition. An ontology of differing/deferring necessarily involves the avowal of inscription always already there, of a pre-inscription revealed after the event and a mourning of presence.

Every *voice, vox,* in as much as, since the Bible, this has been the name borne by the pure actuality of the event, comes to us recorded, phenomenalized, formed and informed, if only in the tissue of spatio-temporal agencies, in the 'forms of sensibility', here and over there, not yet and already no longer, etc. Not to mention the meanings pre-inscribed in the 'language' spoken by the voice.

Plato wrote his dialogues, in the trivial sense of writing. But even if a work of language had remained unwritten, it would none the less have been inscribed even in the oral tradition of the bards, storytellers, which involves no less technique, even if it is a different techniques, than graphics. The universalization of the idea of writing prevent any separation of the act from its placing in reserve, of the living and the dead, the work and its conservation, genius and technique. In his research at the Collège International de Philosophie, on the so-called new technologies and their relation to so-called culture, Bernard Stiegler takes the critique of the prejudice hostile to archiving in the other direction. There is no culture, even so-called archaic culture, which is not sustained by a technique, because culture is always transmission (whether it operates through tradition, institutions or media) and because transmission demands inscription. A thing is cultural because it is exhibited, i.e. inscribed or 'written'. Conversely, Stiegler is able to show that any technique, in so far as it is inscription, is memorization or conservation, far from being a means that would come as an extra to be applied to spontaneous works to ensure their transmission and conservation. And of course he does not mean thereby to run together every kind of technology. But he does at least demand that the new kinds, or 'new technologies', should stop being considered, as they most often are, as new means, applied to works unchanged in their essence.

On the contrary – and I think I can say this in his name – it is the very relation of the mind to time and to space which is displaced by them, from the moment of the operation, of the *opus*. Following this orientation, one must consent without disgust to the institution of the museum, since the upkeep [*entretien*] in the sense of maintaining is not longer to be ascribed solely to deliberate memorization. There is nothing alarming in the fact the archiving of works should take *place* (and moment), especially not painted works, if it is true that any work is already necessarily an archive, a spatio-temporal organization, 'blocked', in some sense, to permit repetition and transmission. Deleuze says 'territorial-

148

ized'. But you know that territoriality can 'engage a movement of absolute deterritorialization', and 'stop being terrestrial and become cosmic'.*

What we can be alarmed about is that the museum might neglect the modes of inscription and organization of space and time that the new technologies are, at the very moment when, in today's version of humanity, they are in the process of replacing the 'old' technology of writing-graphics.

And what we can also be alarmed about is that, whatever the technical mode the museum satisfies, the aspect of archiving and blocking, what I'd call the 'apparatus' in the exhibiting of works might, in their perception and reception, take precedence over the aspect of differing/deferring, of putting back into play, of 'bouncing back', as Buren says. I would say of welcoming the event, and, in our case, that ontological event that colour can be.

That there should necessarily be spatial inscription, trace and conservation in no way entails that the mind is doomed to repetition, and that there is nothing else to inscribe which has not already been inscribed. A despair that is nowadays often adorned with the name of 'new' or 'neo'. I won't develop this fear any further here, and the demand it brings as to the conception and function of the museum. The point is not to collapse them back onto the prejudice I've just denounced, the implication that only the 'live' is any good, or, as the public authorities put it, 'creation'.

I would prefer to end by saying a couple of things about what in my view is the important point. It may seem to contradict what I have just said. I do not think that it does.

You will remember that in trying to make the reader of the 1767 *Salon* see the landscapes painted by Vernet, Diderot pretends in his writing that he is strolling in them with his friend the Abbé. Through writing, he opens the surfaces of the pictures like the doors of an exhibition. As in the museum, it is not just eyes, but whole bodies that come to move, and no longer *in front of* the disposition of colours, but *amidst* them. Each landscape fictively traversed in this way is

*G. Deleuze and F. Guattari, *Mille plateaux* (Paris: Minuit, 1980), pp. 341–433.

the exhibition of a 'nature'. Through this feature, Diderot abolishes – I'd like to say 'abridges' – the opposition of nature to culture (nature is a museum of colours), of reality and the image, of volume and surface.

There would be a lot to say about this procedure. Here I wish only to take it as witness to what I believe to be at stake in painting, and perhaps more so today than recently or long ago. By pointing out that landscapes are exhibitions, Diderot also suggests the opposite, namely that exhibitions are landscapes. It is enough, perhaps, to take the situation of works in museums in itself and for itself, *without referring it* to their supposed initial situation, in the studio, at the moment of the 'first' sketch, or even what might have been the artist's 'first' imagination of them. It is enough to convince oneself that there is not *one* originary freshness, but as many states of freshness as what we might call dis-armed gazes. As many times of presence as there is soul (Kant uses the word in the third *Critique*).

It was in order to support this really quite trivial – too trivial – idea that I started with colour. As opposed to forms, and still more figures, colour appears to be withdrawn, at least through its 'effect', through its potential for affecting feeling, from the circumstances of context, conjuncture and, in general, from any plot [*intrigue*]. This is why it is usually classified, in aesthetic theory, on the side of matter or material. Form (or figure) can always, from near or far, be referred to an intelligible disposition and can thus, in principle, be dominated by the mind. But colour, in its being-there, appears to challenge any deduction. Like the timbre in music, it appears to challenge, and in fact it undoes it. It is this undoing of the capacity for plot that I should like to call *soul*. Far from being mystical, it is, rather, material. It gives rise to an aesthetic 'before' forms. An aesthetic of material presence which is imponderable.

I know very well that colour changes with light, lighting, the weather and the passing of time. But it is because we have given it a name, a place in the table of samples, and because this designator inspires the principle that it is and must always remain the same. But it is its very mutability that makes it propitious for the disarming of the gaze. Everything

150

is changed in the timbre (to keep the musical metaphor), or the fragrance, in olfactory terms, according to whether you open the curtains of the choir of San Francesco d'Arezzo, whose walls bear Piero's frescoes, or whether you direct spotlights onto them. But it cannot be demonstrated that one of these is more 'beautiful' than the other – let's say less 'present' than the other.

I saw in Montreal little landscapes by Vernet himself, under glass and lit by neon, whose livid quality thus obtained had an immediate force of interruption or forbidding of the mind.

The painter is seized or made to let go by a shade. Cézanne in front of his mountain. He tries to transport it onto his support. He knows that he will not be faithful. But what is he attempting at least? To get the looker to feel (let's use this word, for want of a better) the same letting go when faced with the colour posed and composed in the picture. It is not a question of authenticity, which is a market value.

It seems to me that the aim of painting, beyond and by means of all the plots with which it is armed, including the museum, is to render presence, to demand the disarming of the mind. And this has nothing to do with representation. Painting multiplies technical and theoretical plots to outplay or play with representation. It belongs to voluntary memory, to the intelligence, to the mind, to what questions and concludes. But it happens that a yellow, the yellow in Vermeer's view of Delft, can suspend the will and the plot of a Marcel. It is this suspension that I should like to call soul: when the mind breaks into shards (letting go) under the 'effect' of a colour (but is it an effect?). And then one writes twenty or one hundred pages to pick up the pieces, and one puts together the plot again.

Now I see no reason at all why this aim, this unique aim of painting, this material presence, should necessarily fail from the fact that the yellow of the wall is hung up in a museum rather than elsewhere, if it is true that chromatic matter owes nothing to the place it can take (and which in a sense it never takes) in the intrication of sensory positions and intelligible meanings. And this is how the case of a museum of painting is different from others, from many others. Through the fact that it exhibits chromatic matter, which makes an appeal to presence beyond representation. All one can expect from it is for it not to prevent the state of letting go by making itself too prominent.

And finally, so as to avoid confusion, I want to make it clear that when I say colour, I mean any pictural matter, beginning with the line. In the old Japanese calligraphies, the stroke of the brush does not make a line in the sense that a draughtsman's pen does. And what should one say about Yves Klein's imprints?

13

God and the Puppet

Here is the story I would have liked to tell you: that repetition escapes from repetition in order to repeat. That in trying to have itself forgotten, it fixes its forgetting, and thus repeats its absence.

Repetition is a problem of time. And music is a problem of time. But also of sonorous matter. It is said that musical time is the organization or the set of forms 'imprinted' (what a word!) on sonorous matter, on sound. Every organization, every form, spatial as much as temporal, involves its repetition, whether actual or possible. Because it is the fixing of a state of matter through duration, and that fixing demands the recurrence of the organization of the material elements. We also tend to say that sound, matter itself, is analyzable into its parameters: amplitude, period, frequency, duration, resonance. And as we are dealing with the vibratory movement of a gas (air), the nature of this movement and its propagation also imply a repetition, that of the oscillation of the mobile part (for example the reed of an oboe) which draws this movement along. And also the rigidity of the sounding apparatus. Here the formal, or even conceptual, organization, 'descends' into the heart of the sonorous matter.

Two observations on this point. First, the characteristic properties of a sound are in principle measurable, and it is the task of acoustics and the physics of vibrations to determine them quantitatively. But the cognitive identification of sound demands that the oscillation of the mobile part which

153

determines the amplitude, the period, the frequency of the sound remain equal during the observation. The same goes for the sounding apparatus, whatever it is, which ensures the propagation of the sound. Any modification of the apparatus modifies the interferences which contribute to the definition of the basic sound and its harmonics. The determination of the properties of a sound thus demands the exactly identical recurrence of the conditions of its production.

But in fact, the organization of the sets of sounds (thus determined in their identity), i.e. their composition into musical forms, does not only obey the principle of quantitative identity, and therefore of identical repetition. It admits, and probably demands, the variation or the transposition of these forms by means of changes applied to the sound-elements. It demands it because musical pleasure appears to depend on the perception of these differences: at one and the same time the mind enjoys the same through the other, and is enchanted by the diversity that identity accepts. Acoustics is directed towards knowledge, music towards a certain sort of pleasure. They are two different 'genres' of discourse or 'faculties'. I would say in Kantian terms that the exact identification of the sound belongs to the understanding in its cognitive finality, but that the variation of its putting into form comes under the imagination obeying the finality without concepts proper to the disinterested pleasure which, according to Kant, characterizes the aesthetic feeling of the beautiful. So we shall always have to distinguish between the determined and determining repetition which fixes sonorous matter into distinctive properties for acoustic knowledge, and the 'free' repetition (the term is Kantian) of the forms of the musical composition of the sounds with each other.

It is clear that the first-named repetition is guided by an Idea (in the Platonic sense) of a self (the sound) according to its exclusive identity, whereas the second which accepts variation and transposition is 'only' made up of analogy. Which entails, among other things, that the identity of what is repeated is, in this second case, not determined, that it is only indicated as the object of an allusion made to it by the different occurrences of chord or phrase, that each of these occurrences adds to the others a sort of supplement due to its very difference, and that this supplement, which is perhaps (and this is Aristotle rather than Plato) nothing other than art, *techne*, always presupposes the absence or retreat of the thing itself, i.e. of the chord or the phrase to which these occurrences allude. What I mean is that none of these occurrences can stand to any of the others as their paradigm. One does not 'give' the theme of a symphonic movement as one 'gives' the 'A' at the beginning of the concert to tune the instruments. The first repetition, which is cognitive, induces a metaphysics of ideas, and the second, which is aesthetic, an ontology of being as non-being.

The second observation is of a different order. The distinction I have just drawn rests, apparently, on the opposition of a musical matter – sound – subject to temporal (and spatial) conditions, with its composition into forms, which also requires a treatment, albeit a different one, of time. Now this opposition of matter and form, which corresponds to that of a measurable time and a flexible duration, is called into question, or so I believe, by the consideration of timbre, or rather, of the nuance of a sound or a set of sounds. That matter appears to escape determination by concepts because it is rigorously (and not exactly) singular: its quality depends perhaps on a constellation of conceivable parameters, but *this* constellation, the one which takes place now, cannot be anticipated, foreseen. For example, it is this singularity which, at least in part, distinguishes the different performances of the same work. And one is thus tempted to think that it escapes all repetition, not only that involved in constituting the sound's identity, but that of the formal variation demanded by music. Even what is aptly called the 'rehearsal' [*répétition*] of a work by a performer or a group of performers cannot manage to control the timbre or the nuance which will take place, singularly, on the night of the concert. With the nuance, it seems that the ear is given over to something incomparable (and therefore something unrepeatable) in what is called the performance, i.e. to the here and now of the sound, in their singularity, in their one-offness, in the aspect by which they are, by virtue of their position, not subjected to any spatio-temporal transfer. This transfer can consist in no more than the maintenance of the

155

'same' sound in memory for even a short duration – this does not alter the fact that it immediately changes the here into the there, the now into the then. And so the present nuance changes into a nuance reported, retained, deferred, so that it becomes a different nuance.

I know that this idea of a pure, punctual presence, which would, ultimately, be an objection to quantitative (eidetic) repetition as well as to allusive (aesthetic) repetition – that this idea of presence remains highly problematic, and I would even say that it cannot be conceived, or experienced, or felt, at least according to the forms of our sensibility. In other words, there is no subject to refer it to itself, since itself, the I, never stops reiterating its power of synthesizing sensory data (here sounds) through the course of time. How could what constitutively repeats itself grasp the unrepeatable as such? No doubt the nuance, for example of a musical performance, can be reported and as it were circumscribed by its comparison with other performances. But this comparison it made after the event, in a sort of sampling of nuances, well known to the chromatologist – the swathe of colour samples. Or the sound engineer: the series of tests. Record critics' discussions means we have got used to these comparisons over the decades. All of them (the swathe, the collection of tests on magnetic tape, records) require the inscription of the nuance on a spatial support, its archiving. But what the comparison cannot establish is that such-and-such a nuance, in its actuality, its here-and-now of that time, can exercise on a given mind (and not on another) not only the effect of a formal pleasure, which is something quite different, but the power of a loss. For if the pure matter of sound, its nuance, can reach the subject, this is at the cost of surpassing, or 'sub-passing', its capacity for synthetic activity. This would be a definition (a negative one indeed) of matter: what breaks the mind. I mean that if this matter, so tenuous that it is as though immaterial, is not repeatable, this is because by being subjected to its seizure by that matter, the mind is deprived, stripped of its faculty – both aesthetic and intelligent – to bind it, associate it, I'd like to say to narrativize it, and therefore, in one way or another (metaphysical or ontological) to repeat it. The nuance, as non-formalized matter, escapes

156

the syntheses, both of apprehension and of reproduction, which usually see to the grasping of sensory matter to ends of pleasure (through forms), or of knowledge (through schemata and concepts). If there is no subject to refer to itself, i.e. to its power of synthesis, the sensory forms and conceptual operators, so as to refer to *this* nuance, the reason is that sonorous matter which *is* this nuance is there only to the extent that, then and there, the subject is not there. You'll remember that this is how Epicurus circumscribes death: if it's there, I'm not there; so long as I'm there, it's not there. We can understand this alternative as the determination of a limit. This would not yet be sufficient. For it is precisely not a limit *for* the mind: it would have to be there at the moment it is no longer there, it would have to persist, different no doubt, but repeated beyond this limit, for it to be a limit of the mind. The limit can be crossed or liberated [*La limite est franchissable, ou affranchissable*]. But I am speaking, under the name 'nuance', of a frankness [*franchise*]. In recalling the Epicurus text, I do not mean to dramatize things – they don't need it. But I do so at least in order to get across the idea that if, among these 'things', there is one which does not tolerate repetition, it is death, it is matter. The extinction of the subject, of the subject's mirror, of its reflexivity in the usual sense, of its most elementary capacity for synthesis, does not come about within its reflexive temporality, like an interval, even one given over to the subject's loss. The interval and that temporality are themselves suspended on it. I say 'suspended' to mark the fact that there is no mark of this loss on the actively reflexive course of the subject.

If there is no possible repetition of this nuance, this must be because it is not inscribed. Our disappointment when we listen to a recording is directed at the singularity that can't be found. Mind through its syntheses has no access to it. When I say: if it is there, the subject is not there, I mean, by the lack of the subject, that we should not try to think of the 'perception' (what a word!) of this nuance like an inscription on a support. Or, to say it the other way round: that we must try to think a trace which, instead of marking, typing (Lacoue-Labarthe) a passive surface, would destroy it. It does not even mark its absence, in the way that a blank, a white page can signal a dead moment, a pause, a silence in a book of writing, of whatever sort.

It might be thought that, given all this, even the memory of this uninscribed 'trace' must be impossible, and that there will be no means of talking about it, even. I do not think so. Nor did Ernst Bloch, telling in little narratives the *Spuren*, the traces, by which the uninscribable, presence, disables the mind. With the slight difference that in his tradition it is not matter which causes this disarray, but the Unnameable. So that the aim of the thought of presence is not in his work aesthetic in principle, but ethical or 'spiritual'. But it is surely not by chance that this aim disdains using the argumentative genre to exhibit itself, and that it draws from Bloch's finest pen the laconic writing of what in Low Latin were called *narratiunculae*. This is what writing – including musical writing – is looking for: what is not inscribed. I'd like to falsify the value of the prefix 'e' to hear in *écriture* something like a 'scratching' – the old meaning of the root *scri* – *outside of*, outside any support, any apparatus of resonance and reiteration, any concept and any pre-inscribed form. But first of all *outside any support*. The matter I'm talking about, the nuance (colour, timbre) would have to be imagined – but this is already much too heavy – as though it were at one and the same time the event and what it happens to. There would not first be a surface (the whole tradition, heritage, memory) and then this stroke coming to mark it. This mark, if this is the case, will only be remark. And I know that this is how things always are, for the mind which ties times to each other and to itself, making itself the *support of every inscription*. No, it would rather be the flame, the enigma of flame itself. It indicates its support in destroying it. It belies its form. It escapes its resemblance with itself.

I shall now try to argue this escape from repetition again, this time as a teacher of philosophy. I first take up the path opened by Kant towards a phenomenology of time, and therefore of music, the art of time. 'Phenomenology' is the term Kant tries for what will be called Aesthetic in the first *Critique*, i.e. in particular a reflection on time. On this path, my task is to pick out (that's repetitive) how much repetition already enters the description of the most elementary grasp of what Kant calls a phenomenon. In what he calls the apprehension of the phenomenon. It is said to be there, present, now, the French word *maintenant* severely recalling how much *already* and *again*, how much maintenance there is in the least instant. Kant wonders what would happen, without the slightest apprehensive maintenance? It would happen that it would happen [*passer*], and that's all. The 'manifold' of the given – and Kant always understands matter as a 'pure diversity', 'before' any ordering, before any form – this diversity, if it were not retained in any way, would run by, without any framing being able to give an instantaneous grasp of it, even for an instant. The constitution of the present instant, on the contrary, already demands a retention, even a minimal one, of various elements together, their 'constitution', precisely. This microscopic synthesis is already necessary for the slightest appearing. For plunging into the pure manifold and letting oneself be carried along by it would allow nothing to appear to consciousness, nor to disappear from it for that matter, appearing not even taking 'place'. This place is due to a synthesis, that of apprehension, which as it were hems the edges of the pure flow and makes discontinuous the pure continuum of the flow while making continue the pure discontinuity of its supposed elements. In short the river needs a bank if it is to flow. An immobile observatory to make the movement apparent. (You see that we have got into phenomenology.)

Apprehension thus requires a minimal temporal hold. This minimum is of course not measurable. Kant says in the *Critique of Judgement* that it is a non-quantitative magnitude, the object of an 'immediate grasp in an intuition', that it cannot be evaluated mathematically – since every mathematical evaluation presupposes a 'fundamental measure' – that it is evaluated 'absolutely' and 'aesthetically' (understand by that that it is grasped before any concept of number). So however slender the 'pinch' of manifold that apprehension consists in, the fact remains that phenomenology demands it for there to be apprehension and appearance. Husserl was introducing a similar theme with the idea of *Retention*. (It is very difficult to distinguish from this apprehensive synthesis the one Kant calls reproductive, that he assigns to the

159

imagination. It seems that there is already reproduction of the elements of the manifold for their present apprehension to be possible. But I will not discuss here this thorny point in the phenomenology of time.)

Now, urged on by the demon of limits, you're wondering what would come of this paradox: a pinch of manifold whose *ambitus* would make the unity of that manifold imperceptible to consciousness, and therefore unexperiencable (in the sense of phenomenological *Erfahrung*), and which by this fact would leave this very small unit unapparent and unappeared to consciousness. In short, very brief moments, and, as we say so calmly, well below the threshold of perception.

By definition: this question can be followed, but not elaborated following the presuppositions of a phenomenology. Husserl or Kant would say that it is metaphysical, that is aporetic. Leibniz's monadology is indeed a metaphysical (but also physical) way of treating it. What Leibniz calls the monad is in a sense nothing other than a potential for a pinch, a synthesis. Now there are powerful monads and others that are puny: Leibniz calls them 'rich' and 'naked'. This hierarchy is a function of their ability to synthesize the manifold. Rich if they can 'take together', posit together, a lot of elements, poor if it is only (at the limit, always) one by one that they can receive them.

The inscription of the one by one does not even provide a landscape. It is in the thread, as it were, of a pure manifold, which excludes the present in the phenomenological sense, and appearance. And *a fortiori* the landscape. At the other end of the hierarchy, one can, and one must, conceive of a monad that conversely synthesizes in one intuition (as Kant says) the totality of elements (information, if you will) capable of being recorded. Shall we say that there is time for the most naked? No, for lack of the minimum of retention of the manifold. And for the most well–endowed? No more for that, since everything is retained in one go. In both cases, the repetition that 'makes' time, according to its difference or deferral, of course, is lacking. The time of the atom, the time of the god, are not what we (the mind that synthesizes, but not everything) experience as temporality. In the order of temporality, these are the two limits or boundary-posts

160

between which temporality can be thought, and which (at the same time, if I can say that) are not themselves temporal or temporalizing. *Mutatis mutandis*, they are like tautology (*p* is *p*) and contradiction (*p* is not-*p*) for the field of logic: propositions which are indeed propositions, but which exclude any truth calculus (an observation of Wittgenstein's).

In a slightly different spirit from that of Leibniz's monadology, but none the less a related one, Bergson (who indeed sometimes cites Leibniz in support) explains that if one does not have sufficient capacity to retain in one go the 400,000 million vibrations per second of the electro-magnetic field which defines (roughly) the chromatic band of red (but one could take the case of a sound-vibration too, simply it is less impressive in terms of the frequency and thus less pedagogical); if, then, one is condemned to capture only one vibration at once, it will take 25,000 years (about) to register red. And of course, this won't 'look red', but be 400,000 million simple shocks. This is the case, says Bergson, for the 'pure' material point, what Leibniz called the 'naked monad'. One the other hand, Bergson's thought lacks (I may be wrong) the other limit, a description of the time or the non-time in which all the colours vibrate at once, in a single phase to the eyes of the richest monad, the colour of the god.

Let's try to imagine what happens at the two limits if the material element, Kant's 'manifold', is sound. The question is that of the beating or the oscillation which generates what we call sound. For the naked monad which receives only one beat at a time, there is no synthesis of the succession, and thus no beating. It hears only one wave, and it does not know that *it is only* one wave. Shall we say that it forgets those which have passed? No more than the billiard ball forgets the shocks it has received from other balls, if it is true that it can do no more than return (according to the law of the impact of bodies) the shock to which it is subjected at that moment. What it lacks in order to be able to forget is the capacity for synthesizing in a single pinch or grasp (or intuition, to talk Kant's language) two – at least two – successive shocks. Its hardness and polish were conceived and realized precisely to prevent any impression being or remaining marked on it.

161

This 'pure' mechanical impassibility would be transcribed in the order of sound not as a deafness, but as a musical impassibility, at least if we accept that music demands that two sounds at least be and remain associated to form a non-random sound-figure, a chord, a bit of phrase. Deprived of the means of comparing the vibrations between them, deprived of plurality, and thus deprived of repetition, this billiard ball in sound come to take the place of the synthesizing subject would hear, we can imagine, only the matter of sound. Can we say its timbre, its nuance? Yes, but on condition that we imagine the nuance as an absolute sound-cloud, with no relation to any other. Only the mind, a monad endowed with superior synthetic powers, could after the fact sort out the nuances received by the ball, and reconstitute the history of the sound-shocks.

As for Leibniz's God, at the other end of the sound-field, he hears all the sounds in the world, the so-called real world, but also of the other possible worlds, in the same instant. If he is intemporal, this is not for lack of retention, but through excess of synthesis. What appears to the mind (the ear) of humans successively is received in one go by the divine ear. The distinction between the horizontal and the vertical in musical writing, impossible for the naked monad for lack of a support that can be inscribed, is irrelevant for the divine monad for lack of spacing. All the beatings of what we spread out in what we would call the sound-history of the world are received as in a single chord, which has neither beginning nor end, since it is limited by no other possible sound. Perhaps what they call the music of the spheres.

I should prefer to hear in it the music of the Aristotelian Prime Mover, all possible phases perceived in a single phase, which is perpetual or automatic. Melody is excluded from it. Perhaps this celestial music should be imagined on the model of white noise. Or rather, on the model of that originary element of matter, held to itself by a terrible attraction or interaction, that astrophysics today imagines 'before' its explosion into a world and into diachronic time. The music (is it music)? that God hears is this sound in which all the characteristics *of* sounds are collapsed onto each other by an attraction which is no less terrible for our human ears. And

GOD AND THE PUPPET

as the material nucleus, exploding, deploys according to the periodic table (an eminently repetitive inscription) elements classified by atomic number, the multiplicity of possible agglomerates, i.e. bodies – so the initial sound can only let what we call music be heard by exploding and distributing the sounds according to pitch in such a way that with these offspring of the originary sonority there can be discernment of harmonies and combination of melodies – i.e. musical objects. And in both explosions, it is time that is born, opening both the possibility of syntheses and stories.

That may be pure delirium. At least there is some precedent for it in an observation made to the narrator of Kleist's *Puppet Theatre* by the maker of automatic dolls. Nothing, he explains, is closer to infinite divine grace than the mechanism these puppets obey. Deprived of all intention (I'd say, deprived of all capacity for temporal synthesis), the dolls merely place their limbs at the moment as they are ordered, following the law of gravity alone. We see how well this observation accords (if I can say that) with the idea of the billiard ball. And how much repetition understood as imme- diate restitution of a movement (a vibration, if we're dealing with sound) is related to divine automatism in Aristotle's sense, which is the self-sufficiency of the Same.

The grace [*Anmut*, but also *Grazie*] Kleist writes about would be like the freeing of the mind from all diachrony, from all task of synthesis. It is the graciousness due to the sufficiency of the all in one, according to God, or the one in all and for all according to mechanics. One used to say *pure act* [*energeia*], and that demanded the exhaustion of resources, beginning with temporalization, the suspension of the task of actualizing and re-actualizing pasts and futures. And this is why God and the doll have no 'quality', since quality is power.

All music, I think, aspires to this grace. All genuine music. Aspires to exemption from syntheses, forms, becomings, intentions and retentions, from repetition, in a word. Aspires to that unique pinch or that 'pinch' of the unique in which the differentiation of the one and the multiple would not have place or time.

It won't come as news to you that it is none the less condemned to resound and consound. But one can distinguish between two sorts of music: the one where the necessity of resonance and consonance (in the philosophical sense) provides the occasion for the deployment (I do not say the exhibiting, but the magnificent depolyment) of the power to synthesize; and the one where this same necessity, and this very power, are on the contrary felt as impotence and pain. The impotence of holding to a material instant, the pain of an impossible sainthood. We are a long way from the god, the god has exploded, galaxies of resonances flee the *templum sanctum* (where the initial sound sounds) at high speed. No doubt they sing, linking such diverse frequencies, pitches and durations. But what cannot be equalled or repeated does not reside in linkings. It hides and offers itself in every atom of sound, perhaps.

14

Obedience

When Adorno writes in *The Philosophy of the New Music* that 'with the liberation of the material, the possibility of mastering it has increased', we understand that this liberation increases the likelihood of a greater capacity with respect to musical material. The sentence does not say whether this increased capacity is permissible and/or desirable. This is a question we have to ask. The question of what is made possible in music by the new technologies also obliges us to consider and examine the rights and the wishes (desires) that the new technologies can declare in the world of sounds. Rights and wishes which are not necessarily those of the human involved – the composer, the performer, the listener – and which could also be the rights and wishes of the material or the sound. In Adorno's sentence, the expression 'liberation of the material' suggests something of that sort, I think: musical material had and has the right and the desire to emancipate itself from a certain number of guardians that were previously inflicted on it. And the paradox (negative dialectic?) shown up by Adorno's sentence is that, once this desire and this right are declared and recognized – so once the material is 'liberated' – sound (if that's what we're really talking about) can, because of this very fact, and even more so because of it, under the mastery of technique.

And yet – Adorno insists on this in the *Aesthetic Theory* – technique is a constitutive aspect of art. 'It means that the

165

work of art is more than an agglomerate of what exists in fact, and this *more* constitutes its content.'

The work is, and must remain, an enigma, but it also offers a 'determinable figure', 'both rational and abstract', and this figure is technique. So from what has the material, here sound, been 'liberated' which makes 'possible', in all the senses of the word, a greater hold of technique on it? And does this 'liberation' precede, follow, accompany this *more* control over sound supposedly provided by the new technologies? Is the principle suggested by Adorno here that the desire and right to free musical material, or the desire and right that material has to free itself, are fulfilled in proportion with the increase in the capacity to determine that same material rationally? In other words, do the new technologies, which allow a refined, very refined ('rational, abstract') analysis of musical material, also allow its liberation?

The question can be turned around. The double permission is to be read in both senses. First sense: the material is all the freer for being more determinable. That's quite easy to conceive and practise. The number of choices to be made – 'freedom' – increases with the increase in the number of variables one can act on with determinism. Second sense: the material is the more determinable and masterable the more it is freed. This seems harder to grasp: expect in the sense explained by René Thom, namely that every explanation, every precise elaboration of a causality, every determination implies a 'break of causality' in the very act of the explanation. When the physicist expounds a 'law' – or, as they say, an 'effect' – and offers it for verification, he sets the stop-watch to zero and encloses the variable he judges to be relevant in the supposedly uncrossable limits of an insulated system, i.e. one where the other variables are considered not to be pertinent. In this sense the determination of the effect demands its freedom. And in so far as the regulated and repeatable obtaining of this effect is realized in an experimental rig and then in a machine, a 'technical' apparatus, then one can understand that practical mastery over it presupposed its isolation outside the 'context', its freeing from that context, and that this freeing happened first in the perception and thought of the scientist and engineer.

166

So one could say that just as sound can free itself, so technique can master it. And conversely. And this euphoric reciprocity would constitute, in principle, the first possible opening for the meeting of music with contemporary technology.

Having said which, now that this little scholarly exercise is done, I should like to organize the brief reflections which follow around two poles. One is called *Tonkunst*, the art of sound and/or tone, the old germanic word for music, and the other, still German, is called *Gehorsam*, translated as *obéissance*,* but losing thereby the *hören*, the *listening* contained in it, and which should rather be transcribed as *obédience*, in which the Latin *audire* can be heard more clearly, something like *lending one's ear to*, and also *having the ear of*, an *audience* brought or accorded to something that sounds, makes a sound or a tone, *tönt*, and which obliges, has itself obeyed.

Everything I have to show is quite simple: first, that what we call music never stops becoming, or becoming again, an art of sound, a competence *to* sound (for *Kunst* was not simply art in the official sense of the fine arts), that music never stops becoming, or becoming again, the address of sound, sound addressed and adroit, and that it is in this regard that its marriage (for it is no concubinage) with techno-science (it is not only a 'technique' in the sense of a means) should be studied, especially as to the possibilities resulting from it; and secondly, that in becoming, becoming again, this competence and this address in sounds through its coupling with the techno-science of sounds, music reveals a destination (I say *destination* to pick up on a term which covers the whole field of so-called 'aesthetic' reflection from Kant to Heidegger), a destination of listening to listening, an 'obedience' that should perhaps be termed absolute, lending the ear an ear: a destination which in any case exceeds the

---

*Lyotard exploits here the French distinction between *obéissance*, which corresponds to the most common sense of the English 'obedience', and *obédience*, which implies ecclesiastical jurisdiction. (Translators' note)

scope of techno-scientific research envisaged technically, yet thanks to which this obedience is revealed.

First, on *Tonkunst*, the art of sound or tone. Going quickly, from a height, without real competence, I repeat, but as a hasty amateur, I'd say that it has become a commonplace to describe the last few centuries of Western music as a history of the 'liberation' of the material – sound – from the various constraints that it had to respect, either all at once or by turns, in order to make itself musically 'presentable'.

I leave to those more expert than myself the task of describing and explaining these constraints, their questioning and their transformation. It looks as though the task of composers was to go through an anamnesis of what was given them in the name of music. Perhaps as though sound, by means of their research and their inventions, were going through its own anamnesis through the strata of its living musical past. The timbres imposed by classical, baroque, modern instruments; the durations and rhythms measured by the time-signature and counterpoint; pitches defined by modes and scales; even intensities – these regulations transmitted by schools and *conservatoires* appear, not necessarily outdated, far from it, but certainly not necessary. Analyzing them brings out an elementary material, the vibration of air, with its components which are themselves analyzable: frequency, amplitude, duration and other finer ones: colour, attack. Artistic meditation on sound thus converges with acoustic, physical and psycho-physiological research. This attraction prepared for the wedding of contemporary music with those new technologies. Only a mind engaged in this work of anamnesis can, after the event, see the musical habits that have sustained it as constraints, at the same time as they remain what they are – ways in which it can exercise its skill on the universe of sound, and enjoy it.

Here's a childish example of this worry with respect to sound: the discrimination of duration in classical notation by breve, semibreve, crochet, quaver, semiquaver, etc., implies a metronomy of sound-time. It is divided into units of equal measure through the movement of a metronome. In each bar a defined number of sounds is lodged, giving each its own duration by division. The rhythm of the phrase is obtained by

168

marking a group of bars, in two-two time, triple time, and so on.

Counter-example: the score of John Cage and David Tudor's *Mureau* (for magnetic tape, synthesizer and voice) is made up of rectangular fields of arbitrary dimensions; the vocalizations, the phonemes to be uttered are marked by letters of various sizes according to the intensity to be given them. These letters are grouped on the rectangles in sorts of clusters; the time taken to execute the rectangle is given at the top of the page; the performer starts the stop-watch at the beginning and stops when the time indicated is up; it is possible that the performance of the phonemes indicated in the rectangle is not over in time or, on the contrary, that a quicker performance leaves unoccupied time, 'silence' (similar features are certainly to be found in some of the scores of Jean-Charles François).

A procedure of this sort modifies a great deal the sensitivity of the ear (I mean the mind) to rhythm. Put bluntly, you can't dance to this music. The regulating metronome disappears. Its regular movement is replaced by the continuous race of the chronometer, which is started and stopped arbitrarily (the break of causality). Whence the interest of Merce Cunningham's choreographies on or beside Cage's music. The rhythm of the sound is not within the 'natural' or 'cultural' rhythmic capacities of the body. The body's command over 'its' space (or vice versa) by means of movements is thereby unsettled. Rhythm is referred solely to immobile listening, which can then be called interior listening. Like the appearance and disappearance of sun-spots on the chromosphere, or, if you prefer, like Duchamp's *stoppage-étalon*, this non-measured rhythm demands that one wait: what is happening?

Here is an example of what one might understand by the 'liberation' of sound-time from metronomic constraint. Let's broaden the rhythmic register. Edgar Varèse, who was really the founder and first militant of the movement for the 'liberation of sound', in particular through the use of new technologies, explains:

In my work, rhythm comes from the reciprocal and simultaneous effects of independent elements interven-

169

ing at prescribed but irregular intervals.*

He is talking here about the rhythm of the whole work, of a polyphony, if you like, and no longer of a monodic element. In the Western tradition, this rhythm is ruled by counterpoint. Varèse opposes to this the idea of a 'projection' of planes or masses of sound onto each other – a projection in the senses of geometrical or expressive drawing, an idea very close to that of the 'stoppage-étalon':

> When new instruments allow me to write music as I conceive it, the movement of masses of sound and displacements of planes will be clearly perceptible in my work, and will take the place of linear counterpoint. When these masses of sound collide, phenomena of penetration and repulsion will appear to result. Certain transmutations will take place on one plane and will appear to be projected onto others. They will move at different speeds, at a variety of angles. The old conception of melody and polyphony will no longer exist. The whole work will be a melodic totality. It will flow as the river flows. (p. 91)

This could be a description of Pierre Boulez's *Répons*, played in Paris in 1984. Writing about *Intégrales*, first performed in New York in 1925, Varèse clarifies what he means by projection:

> In our musical system we deal with quantities whose values are fixed. In the work I've dreamed of, the values change constantly in relation to a constant. In other words, imagine a series of variations in which the transformations would result from a slight alteration in the form of a function, or else from the transposition of one function into another. (p. 128)

A similar analysis would be required for the pitch of the sound. Varèse introduced factory sirens and birdsong into his

*Edgar Varèse, *Ecrits* (Paris: Bourgois, 1983).

compositions. First sirens in *Amériques*, premièred in 1926, and in *Ionisation* (1934): 'They are written like the trajectories of parabolic and hyperbolic sounds', he comments (p. 150).

He uses the sound-contiuum without being concerned to respect the cutting up of this continuum according to mode and scale. He thus gives new impetus to the questioning of constraints affecting the pitch of sound: search for new modes (already in Debussy), exploration of non-European music, essays in atonalism, attention given to percussion sounds (whose frequency does not hold for lack of a volume of resonance).

In painting, after the exploration of the constraints bearing on the chromatic organization of surfaces, only colour remains (Delaunay's first *Windows* dates from 1911). Similarly in music, the analysis of the regulation of pitch eventually leaves as its remainder only the material, the enigmatic presence of vibration. In a melancholic and irritable text, Pierre Schaeffer writes:

> When there are no longer any rules at all, the time comes for the rule of atonalism. Nothing, but nothing, remains of what went before. And yet there remains sound . . . . And sound is prodigal with huge remains.*

The principle of musical objects proceeds from this purgation. It is tightly correlated with acoustic research. And as for pitch, Varèse, once again, writes in 1936:

> The new musical set-up I envisage will be capable of emitting sounds at any frequency, and will broaden the limits of the lowest and highest registers, whence new organizations of vertical results: chords, their fitting together, their spacing – that is their oxygenation. Not only will the possibilities of the harmonics be revealed in all their splendour, but the use of certain interferences created by partial harmonics will bring appreciable gains. We can also expect to make use of what is

---

* 'L'art d'accommoder les restes', *Silences*, I (September 1985), p. 194.

radically unthought in the lower resultants and differential and additional sounds. An entirely new magic of sounds! (p. 92)

What is 'radically unthought' is unthought of the ear, something inaudible: 'The new musical instrument of today has a greater range which reaches and can pass the limit of what can be heard' (p. 144).

Whence there emerges, according to its necessity, the idea of an 'internal ear'. This 'interiority', already invoked around rhythm, relates to what I have suggested under the heading of obedience.

There would be still more interesting things to sound out: the question of timbre, or that of the form of the work. And still more so the relation of form and timbre. Just a word about this last. Cézanne said that form is accomplished when colour has reached perfection. He was thereby rejecting the classical principle or prejudice of the opposition of form (construction through drawing) and matter (colour applied subsequently to the drawn figures), and of the priority of form over matter. The chromatic matter ought to lay itself out 'of its own accord', as it were. It does not receive a form. It forms form. The chromatic values are laid out without being organized by a concept, even a guiding one. Beauty, if I dare use this term, is obtained through this autotely without *telos*. This is a problematic that should be connected with scientific research on morphogenesis. Varèse makes a similar observation about sound-colour, i.e. timbre:

But the timbres taken one by one, as well as their combination are the necessary ingredients of the sound-mix – they colour and differentiate the various planes and volumes – and far from being the fruit of chance, they are one with form. I do not use sounds on the basis of subjective impressions as the impressionists did when they chose their colours. In my musical works, the sounds are an intrinsic part of the structure. (p. 124)

This autostructuration of colours (Varèse happily uses the metaphor of 'crystallization') implies notably a liberation

172

from the great musical forms accredited by the tradition, and especially the sonata form. Contemporary music undoes the melodic plot in which the sound-matter is subordinated to a sentimental narration, an odyssey. The dialectic of epic which encloses the time of the work in a beginning, a development and an end – with its harmonic counterpart, resolution – stops organizing musical temporality. What is presented in contemporary music is a temporality of sound-events, accepting anachrony or parachrony, rather than a diachrony. This is what Varèse was getting at under the name of 'sound space', tried out in 1958 at the Phillips Pavilion built by Le Corbusier in Brussels. First exhibition of immaterials.

In a text entitled 'The 80's: without utopia' Ivanka Stoïanova quotes Gérard Grisey:

> The concept of development gives way to that of process... The anchoring point of the process is no longer at the beginning of the score: it is diffused in each instantaneous choice, and measured by the degree of pre-audibility....*

I shall say no more about this. The new technologies can (capacity, eventuality) favour this work of anamnesis bearing on the strata of music which separate sound from the ear. Music as *Tonkunst* tries to rid itself of music as *Musik*. Just as psychoanalysis, when it is the real kind, must rid itself of the psychological sciences. Or philosophy, when it manages to be thinking, must rid itself of philosophy. A deep affinity links the techno-science of sound with this work, this *Durcharbeitung*. For this techno-science proceeds, for its part, from an anamnesis which, in the form of a fundamental crisis, has affected the sciences no less than the arts. For a century now, geometry, arithmetic and mechanics have devoted themselves to interrogating and obstinately elaborating their so-called 'proper' objects, i.e. space, time (the ordered series of numbers) and movement respectively. The sciences have in this way gone through, and are still going through, their 'perlaboration', their crossing of strata of

* Ivanka Stoïanova, 'Des années 80: sans utopie', *Silences*, I, 1985

'obvious truths' bequeathed by the mathematical and physical tradition. This cure has been given the unfortunate label of 'crisis of foundations'. Can reason 'construct' – the word used by the Vienna Circle, i.e. account for – the totality of propositions admitted by the systems of space and number, failing which, it will choose as axioms propositions which are indeed not demonstrable, but fruitful for the mind and for knowledge, especially in physics? Or is scientific thought itself forced to introduce, right into the exposition of apparently decided axioms, intuitions of spatio-temporal properties which it can neither eliminate nor deduce without presupposing them? In other words, givens, *data* in the strong sense. As for our subject, the question is clearly this: can one construct time entirely without reference to *listening*? In listening memory close and distant, presence, waiting, fluctuation, a process of forming which is itself fluctuating are played out – in short, all of internal time, the inner sense.

There is *no more than* an analogy, but *there is* an analogy to be thought between the 'crisis of foundations' in geometry, arithmetic and mechanics on the one hand, and, on the other, the questioning of obvious received truths in most of the arts over more than a century – which is designated by another unfortunate name, the movement of avant-gardes. Of course what is at stake is different: it is not the same thing to seek to know the properties of sound and to attempt to engender emotion through sound. Not the same thing, as Kant said, to judge in determinant fashion and to judge in reflective fashion. But if the nature of this emotion stops being prejudged, for example under the name of natural pleasure or of taste, and if for its part science questions these concepts, then nothing is to prevent scientists coming to help the search, by artists, for other, 'unheard of' emotions. Varèse fought against the separation of the arts and the sciences.

He refers to the place than music occupied in the medieval division of the liberal arts:

Medieval philosophers divided the liberal arts into two categories: the *trivium*, or arts of reason applied to language – grammar, rhetoric and dialectic – and the *quadrivium*, or arts of pure reason . . . which nowadays

174

we would call sciences. Music entered into this latter category, alongside mathematics, geometry and astronomy.

Today, people would be inclined to classify music in the arts of the *trivium*. At least it seems to me that too much stress is placed on what could be called the grammar of music.

At various periods and in various places, music has been considered either as an art or as a science. In truth, music belongs to both. At the end of the last century, Jean Wronsky and Camille Durutte, in their *Treatise on Harmony*, had to invent new terms and describe music as 'art-science'; they defined it as 'the incarnation of intelligence as contained in sounds'. (pp. 102–3)

Varèse gives a precise example of this connivance of the concept and the flesh. The use of the (recorded) sound of sirens in several of his works, then of the same sound synthesized in the *Electronic poem* (1985), was suggested to him by reading Helmholtz's *Physiological Theory of Sound*, in which experiments on sirens serve to establish the harmonic theory of timbre. So we see how studying the derivative of a function of the pitch of sound taken as a variable can both contribute to a critique of arithmetical representation of sound and increase the size of the field of sound offered or opened to the composer.

On this point, and in the same spirit, I should like to dissipate a false conflict which has arisen in the arts, particularly in relation to the use of the new technologies. The sciences of space and time are divided on the question of their foundations, between those who defend ultimate intuition, and partisans of axiomatic construction. An analogous split has, perhaps, shaken the arts of space and time. It has been claimed that the alternative, between a strategy of (infratechnological) impoverishment and a strategy of (hypertechnical) enrichment with respect to space-time, is always present for modern and contemporary artists, even if it is not always decisive or decided, not above all resolved. In both cases, the point is to make felt (through feeling, emotion) what is insensible in the spatial and/or temporal sensory field, what is invisible, inaudible. But one can manage to do this, or believe one has managed to, either by default or excess, by going either towards what is most elementary or supposed to be, or towards the most complex (or what is supposed to be).

This opposition is in any case quite different from the dichotomy proposed by Worringer between the arts of *Einfühlung*, friends of the world, and the arts of abstraction, hostile to the world. But above all, it is probably useless if one tries to classify the major 'schools' or the great currents which have divided the avant-gardes. For example, it would be useless to place Minimalism, *arte povera*, happening, performance, Cage, Morton Feldman or Jean-Charles François on the 'poor' side, and on the 'rich' side abstraction, conceptualism, Nono, Boulez, Xenakis, Stockhausen or Grisey. Rather the hesitation between the two, the paradox or the tension can be seen and heard in each one of these works, as is very clear in the work of Maurizio Klagel.

What paradox? If the arts today still are 'arts', this is because they are inscribed in the field which, since Baumgarten and Kant, has been called 'aesthetics', the field of 'presentation' *hic et nunc*. Here, now, a sound sounds, deploying in the ungraspable instant its flight and a wait. There is no music, especially not as *Tonkunst*, without the enigma of this *Darstellung*, immediately transcribed into feeling before any objectivation and therefore, in a sense, before any 'audition', in a sound-feeling which is perhaps the most elementary presence *of* time or *to* time, the 'poorest' degree or state (although it is not a state) of being-time: *Durchlaufen*.

But precisely, this being-now (rather than being-there, *Dasein*), this donation, is quickly forgotten when it is taken up in the tight weave of musical rhetorics (let's say rhetorics rather than grammars) which regulate, if not determine, its occurrence: rhetorics of harmony, melody, instrumentation, and so on.

From this feeling of occurrence, which all contemporary music has in common, two paths can, in principle, appear to open: the 'intuitionist' path (to speak like the philosophers of geometry and arithmetic) and the 'axiomatic' path. The weave which mutes listening is undone, or is supposed to be

176

undone, either by 'letting sound be', as Cage says; or else, on the contrary, by outplaying it by more complex weaves, not so much rhetorical as cognitive, often called 'structures', in which the various dimensions of sound are experimented with, with a view to being made 'present' to sound-feeling. Let's call this the Boulez tendency.

Now this opposition is probably of no use for deciphering works. There is a minimalism of the very complex: all technological mediations come back to the donation of sound 'now'. And there is an inevitable conceptualism even in the writing of 'poor' works, consisting of noises obtained through the percussion of arbitrarily chosen objects: 'qualunquism' in sound demands the greatest reflection and sometimes a true axiomatic. But above all, the opposition between the two currents is illusory. If it is true that in both cases the aim is to return the ear to listening, it is naive to believe that it is enough to make a sound with anything at any moment to obtain the sound-feeling; and it is dangerous and frivolous to privilege technology, whose end is to test cognitive hypotheses bearing on sound and its hearing, the danger consisting in that case in the temptation of a pure experimentation of acoustic possibilities in which the anamnesis of sound-feeling is forgotten on principle (not a rhetorical principle this time, but a scientific one).

To sum up, obedience, if it is indeed with this that we are dealing, is not given, it is to be unveiled in hearing. Deconstructing hearing in no way means returning to some natural state of listening that musical culture has allegedly caused us to lose. But constructing a knowledgeable culture of hearing can have a 'musical' value (in the sense of *Tonkunst*) only if the sound-machines and the exact structurations they demand eventually destine the work to the marvel of the sound-event alone.

It is time to say a word about obedience. It is not the liberation of sound which seems to me to be stake in *Tonkunst*, but that of obedience, or rather respect for obedience.

I know nothing of Emmanuel Swedenborg, the eighteenth-century theosophist who founded the Church of New Jerusalem, except that Kant sharply criticizes his illuminism

177

and prophetism. It is rather by chance that I found the following lines, taken from his *Treatise of Representations and Correspondences* (c.1750):

> The Spirits which correspond to Hearing, or which constitute the province of the Ear, are those which are in simple Obedience: that is those which do not reason to see if a thing is thus, but which, because it is said to be thus by others, believe that it is thus: whence they can be called Obediences. If these spirits are like this, this is because the relation of hearing to language is like that of passive to active, as like the relation of him who hears speech and acquiesces to him who speaks: whence too in common language, 'to listen to someone' is to be obedient: and 'to listen to the voice' is to obey: for the insides of the language of man have for the most part drawn their origin from Correspondence, for the reason that the human spirit is among the spirits which are in the other life, and it is there that it thinks; man is absolutely ignorant of this, and corporeal man does not even want to know it . . . .

Auf jemanden hören, to listen to someone, to lend one's ear to someone, *das ist gehorsam zu sein,* is to be of obedience (I'm inventing the German – Swedenborg's *Treatise* is written in Latin). To obey is *gehorchen. Gehören* is not far, to pertain to, to depend on an agency, to fall into a domain, under an authority, a *dominus.* And *zuhören,* to lend one's ear. There is an inexhaustible network linking listening to belonging, to the sense of obligation, a passivity I should like to translate as *passibility.*

And what is remarkable in this text is that first, this obedience is that of spirit to spirit, it is a convocation by another voice, it belongs to what Swedenborg calls 'the correspondence between spirits', to a spiritual message-network; and secondly, that man knows nothing, and wants to know nothing, of this dependence of the ear on the spirit, of this taking hostage of hearing by the beyond of the body.

It is possible to read this text, and probably Swedenborg in general, laughing at a man who 'hears voices', i.e., when no-one is talking. On the other hand one can understand him to be designating precisely the essential features of what there is to be 'liberated' in sound, and in particular the essential features of what music aided by contemporary technologies is trying to free in sound, its authority, the belonging of the spirit to the temporal blowing-up involved in the 'being-now' of the heard sound.

I didn't quite tell the truth when I said that I had come across Swedenborg's text by chance. I was led to it by a remark of Giacinto Scelsi, taken from a little text called 'The Look of the Night', itself extracted from his book *Sound and Music*. (Look of the night: Swedenborg wrote, 'To the insides of the Ear belong [*gehören*?] those who have a sight of internal hearing.' That's the nocturnal look, the listening eye.)

The remark in question is as follows:

Yes, it is true that there is also another music of a transcendental character which escapes all analysis of its organization, as it escapes all human understanding. Certain privileged beings have heard sounds, melodies and harmonies that can be described as 'out of this world', just as there are colours belonging to the same plane. In the writings of the Saints there are large numbers of narratives and a whole literature and iconography resulting from it; musical angels with trumpets, lyres and flutes: the narratives of Swedenborg or Jacob Boehme about marvellous music heard by them, and sometimes by whole crowds in different places . . . .*

This remark is part of a vigorous critique of the attention Western classical music reserves principally for the 'musical frame, what one calls musical form'. Scelsi protests that this frame, even in the case of the greatest – Bach, Beethoven, Mozart – can remain empty inside. And he concludes:

* *Silences*, II (1985), p. 84.

179

You want me to tell you that the music of Bach or Mozart would not have been capable of bringing down the walls of Jericho? Yes, that's about it.

The request formulated by Jean-Claude Eloy in his interview with Aimée-Catherine Deloche would move in the same direction, or at least in an analogous direction – the request that music be made not with 'notes in an intervallic relation' (as, according to him, is Boulez's), but with 'quite complex, very condensed sounds . . . , clusters given an inner life, a mobility, beats, harmonics, slowings-up', sounds that he finds an example of in Indian musics, in Ravi Shankar, in Ram Narayan, but which can be obtained electronically, and which he calls 'meditation sounds'. It appears that their wealth is formulated in an apparently Minimalist ideal, in the laconic nature of 'Japanese sound': '*A little water in a garden*'.

I am going to stop, although everything remains to be said, for this little water never stops arriving, running up, or better, occurring. I should have liked to approach the problem from its energetical angle, and that is necessary, given that the new musical technologies are in a sense nothing other than transformers of informational, i.e. electronic energy into mechanical energy, here into vibrations of air and ear-drum, retransformed into nerve-input. Scrupulous meditation demands that this influx not be spent in reanimating bodily mechanics. François Bayle suggests this sharply in connection with musical research:

> Finally, the question of the excluded body (attention: excluded from the field, but present and the more present for its absence: in fact, the body in the margin. omnipresent, found anew).*

It is at this price, the price of this ascesis, that the *Tonkunst* can make the walls of Jericho fall, the walls of our body, with their demands accredited by custom, and their haste towards early satisfactions.

* 'Pro-positions', in *Silences*, I, p. 103.

With these walls, a whole anthropology of sound falls. The obedience revealed for a moment in *Tonkunst* (with or within new technology) means that we (who, we?) are due to the donation of the event. This request is ontological, as it were; no-one is asking us anything.

15

Scapeland

Cast down the walls. Breach and breathe. Inhalation. BREATH, inside and outside. This concerns the thorax. The muscular walls of the rib-cage, of the defences of the thorax, exposed to the winds. Your breath has been set free, not taken away. An understatement: mouth to mouth contact with distance, as though with an infinity of air. And because the walls are down, there is no swelling.

Vesania or 'systematic' madness: 'The soul is transferred to a quite different standpoint, so to speak, and from it sees all objects differently. It is displaced from the *sensorium communi* that is required for the unity of (animal) *life*, to a point far removed from it (hence the word *Verrüchung*) – just as a mountainous landscape sketched from an aerial perspective calls forth a quite different judgement when it is viewed from the plain.'* Conversely, for the bird, the rat that dwells on the plain must also be systematically mad, a landscape-artist, an other alienated, an other estranged. Breathing and breaching the walls of the cage are not, then, the main point. For the bird, the mole's myopic tunnels would mean distance, and would be a landscape which abolishes limits. A burrow in which it is impossible to see anything, impossible to breathe. No one element (an aura, a breeze) is privileged over any

*Immanual Kant, *Anthropology from a Pragmatic Point of View*, tr. Mary J. Gregor (The Hague: Martinus Nijhoff, 1974) 54, 4.

other. There would appear to be a landscape whenever the mind is transported from one sensible matter to another, but retains the sensorial organization appropriate to the first, or at least a memory of it. The earth seen from the moon for a terrestrial. The countryside for the townsman; the city for the farmer. ESTRANGEMENT [*dépaysement*] would appear to be a precondition for landscape.

A stretch of road lined with poplars at midday, made strange by the light of a full summer moon a few years ago at about eleven at night when Mars was in conjunction with Venus. Baruchello calls me from Rome to ask if I've seen the wonderful sky. Theatrical lighting engineers understand LIGHT's function in painting a landscape. So do the Impressionists. And Rembrandt, when it comes to shadows.

Losing oneself in a world of sound. Hearing breaks down the defences of the harmonic and melodic ear, and becomes aware of TIMBRE alone. And then we have the landscape of Beethoven's late quartets.

Infinity: inexhaustible resources are required if there is to be any landscape. 'A palace is not worth living in if you know its every room', writes Lampedusa. A burrow is like that palace; habitable because it is UNINHABITABLE.

The opposite of a place. If place is cognate with destination. See Aristotle. Landscape as a place without a DESTINY. Apply J.- L. Déotte's argument about works of art to the object known as 'landscape'; when they are hung in a museum, works of art are stripped of their destination (be it mythical, religious or political). They are exhibited in their visible presence, here and now. A cove, a mountain lake, a canal in the metropolis can be hung short of any destination, human or divine, and left there. When they are hung in this way, their 'condition' is impalpable, unanswerable. The grey that drifts over the sea after a storm. It is not that you get lost in them, but that their meanings are lost. Foreign capitals visited for the first time. The darkness of all the Rembrandts in the Metropolitan Museum in New York dazzles you as soon as you enter the room. A very long time ago when I was very small; the port of Amsterdam; rails and points encrusted into the cobbles on the quayside; the mist lit from behind by the rising sun like a gauze, and through it I watch the elephantine liners and freighters ruminating, as though they had been stabled in a thousand docks.

Deserts, mountains and plains, ruins, oceans and skies enjoy a privileged status in landscape-painting, rather as though they were by definition without any destiny. And they are therefore disconcerting [*dépaysant*]. This exclusivity is not to be trusted. Meaning soon gives its orphans a new destination (if only for love of landscape). No, landscape has no elective place in these non-places. But the absence of place threatens them, just as it threatens any possible place. Indeterminacy exercises a gentle violence over the determinate, so as to make it give up its QUOD. And it is not I, nor anyone, who begets this non-place.

A sumptuous banister of ebony, smooth to the touch, decorated with Jugendstyl flowers, winding up continuously and without any visible joints to the fourth floor of a block in East Berlin, a block that stands on a boulevard lined by two avenues of bare black trees – it is January – and which is flanked by other blocks in the same style; the streetlights do little to ward off the gathering darkness; deserted, out of the way, and lonely; we are going to visit a colleague and to take him some banned books. That banister has all it takes to make it a non-place as we climb the stairs. And the feeling of strangeness persists over the coffee and cakes in the bottle-green apartment where the lamps are turned down low, and where our voices are low, but violent. The unreality of landscapes as the saying goes. For a brief moment they unmask themselves as CLANDESTINE. And basically, you never see them again. Try as you may. It is always the unknown room in the palace. The corridor in *If It Die . . .* , or in the burrow.

The FACE, but not the countenance, is a landscape, several landscapes. A photograph of Beckett at eighty. An entire land parched with drought, the flesh defied. And in the wrinkles, in the creases where the pupils flash with anger, a cheerful incredulity. So the mummy is still alive. Just. The network of cracks and furrows represents so many weak points; misery has entered them, infiltrated them and has been welcomed. Waiting for rain.

MYOPIA has one advantage. Always the possibility of two distances; with or without glasses. As though the ear could filter a landscape of sound in two ways. Albertine's cheek as I draw near to kiss it. The smoothness of the forbidden expanse is transubstantiated into oily granules. The eyes' lenses are too convex, and if I touch the skin they make it echo with a stereognostic, chromatic timbre. These landscapes of the flesh are the limits within which you can walk. You never reach the end. Draw back. 'A quite different judgement.'

It is the same with teeth. Landscapes could be classified in terms of how easily they can be nibbled, BITTEN. It would take a bite of tungsten steel to savour the frozen flesh of the lakes of Minnesota in the bitter cold or the Rimouski shore in winter. Given that we don't have that bite, that different judgement, we draw back. But as we do so, we still evoke that impracticable ordeal.

The walls will never be really cast down. Hence the MELANCHOLIA of all landscapes. We owe them a debt. They immediately demand the deflagration of the mind, and they obtain it immediately. Without it, they would be places, not landscapes. And yet the mind never burns enough.

It is a question of MATTER. Matter is that element in the datum which has no destiny. Forms domesticate it, make it consumable. Especially visual perspectives, and modes and scales of sound. Forms of sensibility which have come under the control of the understanding without difficulty. Things are less clear when it comes to their lower sisters who smell, drink in and touch. For a beautiful visual landscape, walking without any goal, strolling and the desire to wander simply authorize a transfer of material powers to scents, to the tactile quality of the ground, of walls, of plants. Your foot savours the morbidezza of the mossy heathland and the undergrowth which flank and contradict the sharp stones of the path. In New York, the cars hurtle down Forty-third Street towards SoHo, crossing the ruts that criss-cross the street in every direction, their back ends bobbing up and down like badly moored rubber boats. They make the ground ring with the hollow sound of a percussion instrument; their tyres make the noise of suckers being pulled off the road. So many untameable states of matter.

It used to be said that landscapes – *pagus*, those border-lands where matter offers itself up in a raw state before being tamed – were wild because they were, in Northern Europe, always forests. FORIS, outside. Beyond the pale, beyond the cultivated land, beyond the realm of form. Estrangement procures an inner feeling of being outside thanks to an intimist exoticism. In cities, in minds. States of mind are states of spiritual matter. Suspended between two mental intrigues. See Rimbaud. Beside himself.

Whether or not you 'like' a landscape is unimportant. It does not ask you for your opinion. If it is there, your opinion counts as nothing. A landscape leaves the mind DESOLATE. It makes lymph (the soul) flow, not blood. You do not associate. No more synthesis. It doesn't follow on. Leave it for later. You pray to heaven, to provide for you in your wretchedness. The wretchedness of a soul rubbed raw by the tiderace of matter.

A lonely traveller, a lonely walker. It is not only that conversation, even conversations with yourself, and the intrigue of desires and understanding have to be silenced. As in a temple, a TEMPLUM, a neutralized space-time where it is certain that something – but what? – might perhaps happen. (What I mean is that this 'templation' is the price that has to be paid so that even the cacophony of the Place de la République can become a landscape at 5.30 p.m. on a winter's day, when it is choked with thousands of jammed vehicles.) Not only solitude, but the disconcertment of the powers, and therefore the defences, of the mind. Not alone with oneself, but behind oneself. The self is left behind, sloughed off, definitely too conventional, too sure of itself and over-arrogant in the way it puts things into scale. It is tempting to speak, yet again, of what Cézanne calls 'little sensations'. Inner desolation.

There are a thousand ways of obtaining this surrender. Feasting or fasting, tobacco, grass, *farniente*, overwork. But it always requires something that is TOO . . . (if only too little). In order to have a feel for landscape you have to lose your feeling of place. A place is natural, a crossroads for the kingdoms and for homo sapiens. The mineral, vegetable and animal kingdoms are ordered by knowledge, and knowledge takes to them quite spontaneously. They are made, selected for one another. But a landscape is an excess of presence. My *savoir-vivre* is not enough. A glimpse of the inhuman, and/or of an unclean non-world [*l'immonde*]. Is this still a form of order, a different form of order, as Kant suggests in his vesania? A displacement of the vanishing point? A vanishing of a standpoint, rather.

We should describe, succeed in describing. Find a rhythm for the sentences, choose the words on the basis of their specific deviation from phonetic and lexical habits, rework conventional syntax. Get closer to singularity, to the ephemeral. But perhaps it is impossible to describe with any spiritual accuracy, with any accuracy of the soul (I will not even speak of feelings) without recounting how, where and when it happened. Without supplying a framework. For it is at this point, one might think, that landscape's power to dissolve really makes itself felt in the sense that it interrupts narratives. If that is the case, we are not looking for a lexical or phonetic opposition, but for an opposition between two genres, between telling and showing, and they are different tenses. But the opposition is therefore not an opposition. Mind finds its poise, its repose in narrative activity. What I mean is this: it establishes, despite the most intriguing artifices, its persistence, its grip and its hold on time. It makes time pass, even fly, but it also holds it back, turns it back, makes it curl into spirals, makes it escape itself and catch up with itself. Whereas landscape simply seizes it. What we call description is no more than a literary procedure which puts mental activity on a par with its narrative stance, and difference is reduced to the *shifting* of temporal indicators (pronouns, verbal tenses, adverbs, etc.). An operationalist reduction of what is 'in reality' (?) an ontological abyss. I am not saying that it has no pertinence; how could we capture the breath of wind that sweeps the mind into the void when the landscape arrives, if not in the texture of the written word? But despite, or beneath, this conscientious approach, we must bear in mind that telling and 'showing' are not two mental positions, or that, if they are, it is only because we forget that they are incommensurate, that showing (the landscape) is already of the order of a reprise or a takeover, that the mind draws itself up when it draws a landscape, but that the landscape has 'already' drawn its forces up against the mind, and that in drawing them up, it has broken and deposed the mind (as one deposes a sovereign), made it vomit itself up towards the nothingness of being-there. In description, writing tries to meet the challenge of being equal to its momentary absence. Not only is it always too late (nostalgia); words themselves are outrageously cumbersome, that is, at once too wretched and arrogant to designate the superplenitude of this void state (melancholia; we will always owe landscape a debt; impossible mourning). Poetry arises out of this understanding of wretchedness; otherwise it is merely a staging [*mise en scène*] and a mobilization [*mise en oeuvre*] of the powers of language. It is the writing [*écriture*] of the impossible description; DESCRIPTURE [*décriture*]. And the difference between describing and recounting should not be confused with deferring, which is the fate that awaits the mind when it tries to grasp itself through logic, theory of knowledge or of literature, narrative or essays. It is matter as landscape that is at stake in poetic descripture, and not the forms in which it can be inscribed. Poetry tries not to tame the forms which form language, not to procure the inscription which retains the event of the landscape. It tries to slip by before its withdrawal.

We therefore have to correct ourselves again, constantly: it is not estrangement which procures landscape. It is the other way around. And the estrangement that landscape procures does not result from the transfer of a sensorial organization into another sensorium, such as the transfer of the fragrance of scents into the flagrance of colours or into the light of timbres. This estrangement is absolute; it is the implosion of forms themselves, and forms are mind. A landscape is a mark, and it (but not the mark it makes and leaves) should be thought of, not as an inscription, but as the erasure of a support. If anything remains, it is an absence which stands as a sign of a horrifying presence in which mind FAILS and misses its aim. Fails, not because it was looking for itself and did not find itself, but (we are forced to fall back on comparisons) in the sense that one can say that one missed one's footing and fell, or that one's legs gave way, as one sits on a bench, watching a window which is lit up but empty.

A baby must see its MOTHER's face as a landscape. Not because its mouth, fingers and gaze move over it as it blindly grasps and sucks, smiles, cries and whimpers. Nor because it is 'in symbiosis' with her, as the saying goes. Too much activity on the one hand, too much connivance on the other. We should assume, rather, that the face is indescribable for the baby. It will have forgotten it, because it will not have been inscribed. If there is an element of the 'too' involved, it is because there is too much of a mark, rather too much support. The first act in the 'deferred action' Freud tried to elaborate. But he was too much of a psychologist. This mother is a mother who is a timbre 'before' it sounds, who is there 'before' the coordinates of sound, before destiny.

Anyone who asks me, 'Where does your landscape take place?' is prescribing me a topography and a chronography of the mark that is landscape. And yet it is clear that landscapes do not come together to make up a history and a geography. They do not make up anything; they scarcely come together at all. Can it even claimed that they have a family likeness? But although its boundaries are indefinable (how far does kinship extend?; the institution decides), a family is localized

189

(its members live under the same roof), articulated (in terms of categories: father, daughter, maternal cousin, etc.) and may be hierarchically organized (a family tree) around an arbitrarily chosen centre (*ego*). It is not the same with landscapes; they may display no likeness, may date from different epochs, and so on. It is said that they are the product of an imaginary space-time. I think that they have nothing to do with the imagination in the normal sense of the word (which includes Lacan's sense), or with even a free synthesis of forms. Where and when they happen is not signalled. They are half seen, half touched, and they blind and anaesthetize. A PLAINT of matter (of the soul), about the nets in which the mind incarcerates it.

It is only 'after' it has been a landscape, but also while it is still a landscape, that the face is covered over by a countenance and uncovers the countenance. The INNOCENCE of walking in it is forgotten. Prescriptions begin to come and go between you and me. The law takes a grip on the gaze, the nose, the face, the forehead, the joints between the maxillaries and the parietal bones, and the cervical supports of the cranium. Features have to be deciphered, read and understood like ideograms. Only the hair, and the light that emanates from the skin escape its discipline. The law sends signals across what was once a landscape, between its remains; indignation, supplication, distress, welcome, disgust, abandon. It says: Come, Wait, You cannot, Listen, I beg you, Go, Get out. When tragedy steps on to the stage of the passions and of debts, it empties the landscape. And yet, if you ever happen to be in love, really in love, the vista of the face continues to grip you even as you bow to the law that emanates from the countenance. And that is why you no longer know where you are. Too innocent for love if you experience only a defeat due to the excess of presence; too cunning if you only try to obey its peremptoriness. What comes from the other in love is no mere demand. In obedience to the imperative of dependency, and even without the beloved knowing it, the nothingness of the landscape that is his/her face wreaks a very different desolation on your mind. You are no longer simply its hostage, but its lost traveller.

16

Domus and the Megalopolis

The representation of a facade. Fairly wide, not necessarily high. Lots of windows and doors, yet blind. As it does not look at the visitor, so it does not expect the visitor's look. What is it turned towards? Not much activity. Let's suppose that it's pretty hot outside. The courtyard is surrounded by walls and farm buildings. A large tree of some kind, willow, horse chestnut, lime, a clump of pines. Dovecots, swallows. The child raises its eyes. Say it's seven o'clock in the evening. Onto the kitchen table arrive in their place the milk, the basket of eggs, the skinned rabbit. Then each of the *fruges* goes to its destination, the dairy, the cool scullery, the cooking pot, the shelf. The men come home. Glasses of fresh wine. A cross is made in the middle of the large loaf. Supper. Who will get up to serve out? Common time, common sense, common place. That of the *domus*, that of its representation, mine, here.

There are varieties of the common place, cottage, manor. The ostentation of the facades. The commoners move around at a distance from the masters' residences. In place of pastures and ploughed fields, parks and pleasant gardens offer themselves to the facade. Pleasure and work divide space-time and are shared out among the bodies. It's a serious question, a historian's or sociologist's question, this division. But basically, extended or not, divided or not in its exploitation, the basis remains domestic. It is the sphere of reference of the estate, a monad. A mode of space, time

191

and body under the regime (of) nature. A state of mind, of perception, of memory confined to its limits, but where the universe is represented. It is the secret of the façades. Similarly with action. The *fruges* are obtained by nature and from nature. They produce, destroy and reproduce themselves stubbornly and according to the order of things. According to nature's care for itself, which is called frugality. *Alla domenica, domus* gives thanks for what has taken place and had its moment and prays for what will take place and have its moment. The temporal regime of the *domus* is rhythm or rhyme.

Domestic language is rhythmic. There are stories: the generations, the locality, the seasons, wisdom and madness. The story makes beginning and end rhyme, scars over the interruptions. Everyone in the house finds their place and their name here, and the episodes annexed. Their births and deaths are also inscribed, will be inscribed in the circle of things and souls with them. You are dependent on God, on nature. All you do is serve the will, unknown and well known, of *physis*, place yourself in the service of its urge, of the *phyein* which urges living matter to grow, decrease and grow again. This service is called labour. (With the dubious wish, sometimes, to profit also, that the estate should profit, from growth? One wonders. Rhythmed wisdom protects itself agains *pleonexia*, the delirium of a growth with no return, a story with no pause for breath.)

Ancilla, the female servant. From *ambi* and *colere, ambicilla*, she who turns all the way round, the old sense of *colere*, to cultivate, to surround with care. Culture has two meanings: cult of the gods, but the gods also *colunt domum*, cultivate the dwelling, they surround it with their care, cultivate it with their circumspection. The female servant protects the mistress, for to serve is to keep. When she gets up to serve at table, it is the nature-god who cultivates the house, is content there, is at home. The domestic space is entwined and intertwined with circumvolutions, with the comings and goings of conversations. Service is given and returned without any contract. Natural duties and rights. I find it hard to believe that this organic life was the 'primitive form of exchange', as Mauss put it.

192

It is a community of work. It does not cease to work. It works its works itself. These operate and are distributed spontaneously, out of custom. The child is one of these works, the first, the first-fruit, the *offspring*. The child will bear fruit. Within the domestic rhythm, it is the moment, the suspension of beginning again, the seed. It is what will have been. It is the surprise, the story starting over again. Speechless, *infans*, it will babble, speak, tell stories, will have told stories, will have stories told about it, will have had stories told about it. The common work is the *domus* itself, in other words the community. It is the work of a repeated domestication. Custom domesticates time, including the time of incidents and accidents, and also space, even the border regions. Memory is inscribed not only in narratives, but in gestures, in the body's mannerisms. And the narratives are like gestures, related to gestures, places, proper names. The stories speak themselves on their own. They are language honouring the house, and the house serving language. The bodies make a pause, and speech takes over from them indoors, in the fields, in the middle of the woods. Such rich Hours, even those of the poor. The past repeats itself in work. It is fixed, which is to say it is held back and forgotten, in legends. The *domus* is the space-time of this reiteration.

Exclusion is not essential to the domestic monad. The poor man, the solitary traveller, has a place at the table. Let him give his opinions, show his talent, tell his story. People get up for him, too. Brief silence, an angel is passing. Be careful. What if he were a messenger? Then they will make sure he is remembered, domesticated.

Bucolic tableau. *Boukolein* does not only mean keeping the flock. Keeping humans, too, serving them. Yet the *domus* has a bucolic air only from outside, from afar, from the city. The city spends centuries, millenia slowly gnawing away at the *domus* and its community. The political city, imperial or republican, then the city of economic affairs, today the megalopolis spread out over what used to be the countryside. It stifles and reduces *res domesticae*, turns them over to tourism and vacation. It knows only the residence [*domicile*]. It provides residences for the presidents of families, the *domini*, it bends them to egalitarian citizenship, to the workforce and to another memory, the public archive, which is written, mechanographically operated, electronic. It does surveys of the estates and disperses their order. It breaks up god-nature, its returns, its times of offering and reward. With another regulation of space-time set in place, it is in relation to this that the bucolic regime is perceived as a melancholic survival. Sad tropics seen from the north.

A savouring of the sounds. Come from the near distance, the depths of the stables, cacklings, a silence hollowed out round the call of the owls when Venus shines out at dusk, crackling of the alder branches thrown onto the hearth, clogs on the thresholds, conversation on the hill opposite, wasps round the melon, shouts of encouragement to the autumn oxen, swifts madly chasing each other around the darkening roofs. The sounds are toned to the measure of the bitter-sweet, the smoky, the tastelessness of the boiled beans, the pungent dung, the ferment of the hot straw. The tones eat each other up. The minor senses were honoured in the physical *domus*.

What I say about it, the domestic community, can be understood only from where I speak, the human world become megalopolis. From after the death of Virgil. From after the end of the houses. [At the end of the *Buddenbrooks*.] Now that we have to gain time and space, gain with and against them, gain or earn our livings. When the regulation of things, humans and capacities happens exclusively between humans, with no nature to serve, according to the principle of a generalized exchange aiming for more .... In the 'pragmatic' busyness, which disperses the ancient domestic monads and hands over the care for memory to the anonymity of archives. No-one's memory, without custom, or story or rhythm. A memory controlled by the principle of reason, which despises tradition, where everyone seeks and will find as best s/he can the information needed to make a living, which makes no sense [*ne rime à rien*]. The birth of individualities amid dispersion, as Marx said, of singularities in liberty, according to Nancy. The estate façades still standing, because we conserve them, attest to the old, absent *ethos*. Cracked as they are by radiation and telecom-

194

munications. Businesses that they are by means of interfacing.

We know all that by heart, sick of it, today. This slow retreat of domestic, neolithic life, we know what does indeed have to be named, from here, the revolution of the spatiotemporal regime of being-together. Not too difficult, doubtless, to show that Heidegger's *Gestell* is thought only, in return, through the conservation of an idea of service, which is domestic. Which does not only, to a large extent, lead to the motif of his *Dichtung* filtered through Hölderlin, but to the *Dienst* divided into three (the service of thinking, war and work, as in Dumézil) deployed by the *Rectorship Address*. So we know how much our melancholy for the *domus* is relative to its loss. Even Greek tragedy, that enigma, must, we know, be decoded by means of the grid of de-domination, de-domestication. The new law, that of the *polis* and its right. *Themis* goes beyond the ancestral domestic regulation of the *genos*. But this historico-sociological account does not acquit us of tragedy. Our distance, our anti-domestic violence, makes discernible another scene in the tableau of the houses.

In this scene, the female servant with the heart of gold is impure. The service is suspect, ironic. The common work is haunted by disaster. The respect is feigned, the hospitality despotic, common sense obsessed by the banishing of the mad, its burial within. Something remains untamed in the domination, and capable of interrupting the cycles. The domestic monad is torn, full of stories and scenes, haunted by secrets. Acts of violence stretch it to breaking point, inexplicable injustices, refused offers of affection, lies, seductions accepted and unbearable, petty thefts, lusts. Freud makes us reread, via Sophocles and Shakespeare, the tragedy of the Greek families in this penumbra of madness. The generous purposiveness of the god-nature, dressed up by the philosophers with the name of love, reconciliation, being-together as a whole, everyone in their place, of which the *domus* is the wise figure, the awaited birth and the beautiful death, all this is cracked by evil. An evil not even committed. An evil before evil, a pain both more ancient and younger than the sufferings experienced. A pain always new. In the lowest depths of the *domus*, rumour of anti-nature, threat of *stasis*, of sedition.

195

Father, mother, child, female servant with the heart of gold, niece, old man-servant, shepherd and ploughman, gardener, cook, all the figures of wisdom, the corner of the park under the fig tree, the little passage for whispering, the attic and its chests – everything is matter for obscene crimes. Something in the *domus* did not want the bucolic.

Something does not want this recurrent inscription, and it isn't *me*. But as to its place in the domestic hegemony, there the ego does want its share in memory, to make and remake its place in space-time and in the narrative. The son to become the *dominus*, in his turn. The daughter, the *domina*. And the man-servant, of course, the master, here or elsewhere. As long as it's that, in other words the business and busyness of the ego, the ambivalences, hesitations and contradictions, the little ruses and strategies, then domestic nature remains untouched. It pursues its ends through intrigue, it can repair, it will repair. It will inscribe that in its memory, an episode in caution, in conservation. But the rest? What is not resolved in sacrifice, in offering, in being received? The prodigal, the dissipated, the fury? That is not a member of the domestic organism, that is banished into its entrials.

Even more than the city, the republic or even the flabby and permissive association of interests and opinions called contemporary society – it is strange that, even more than with any of these states of assembling the diverse, the *domus* gives the untameable a chance to appear. As though the god-nature which cultivates it were doubling himself with an anti-god, an anti-nature, desperate to make the bucolic lie. The violence I am speaking of exceeds ordinary war and economic and social crisis. Conversely, and in spite of their generality, or because of it, crisis and war do not become desperate unless they are infiltrated with the breath and the asphyxia of the domestic. Even if the houses have long been ruined, it is enough to activate the memory of a lost domain and legend (a living common space, the myth of a pure common origin) for the political and economic community to parade and parody itself as a *gens*, as a *domus* mocked. So then conflict, crisis change into *stasis* and *seditio*, as though they were affecting some domestic *habitus* that had been thought

196

abandoned. The undominated, the untamed, in earlier times concealed in the *domus*, is unleashed in the *homo politicus* and *economicus* but under the ancient aegis of service, *Dienst*. It's necessary, one might say, that shareable matter be densified to the narrow scale of domesticity for anti-matter to deliver its hatred from each body. *Homo re-domesticus* in power kills in the street shouting 'You are not one of ours.' He takes the visitor hostage. He persecutes anything that migrates. He hides it away in his cellars, reduces it to ashes in the furthest ends of his lowlands. It is not war – he devastates. *Hybris* break apart the domestic *modus*. And the domestic remodelling will have served to unleash *hybris*.

The ruin of the *domus* makes possible this fury, which it contained, and which is exercised in its name. But apart from this case, the case of evil, I find it hard to think that in general the emancipation of singularities from out of domestic space-time favours, on its own, freedom of thought. Perhaps thinking's lot is just to bear witness to the rest, to the untameable, to what is incommensurable with it. But to say witness is to say trace, and to say trace is to say inscription. *Retention*, dwelling. Now all memory makes a work. So that at the very moment when thought bears witness that the *domus* has become impossible, and that the façade is indeed blind, it starts appealing to the house and to the work, in which it inscribes this witnessing. And the fact that there are many houses in the megalopolis nowadays does not mean that there are no longer any works, nor any works to be produced. It means that works are destined to be left idle, deprived of facades, effaced by their heaping up. Libraries, museums: their richness is in fact the misery of the great conglomerates of council flats. The *domus* remains, remains as impossible. My common place. But *impossible* is not only the opposite of *possible*, it is a case of it, the *zero* case.

We wake up and we are not happy. No question of remaking a real new house. But no question either of stifling the old childhood which murmurs at our waking. Thinking awakens in the middle of it, from the middle of very old words, loaded with a thousand domesticities. Our servants, our masters. To think, which is to write, means to awaken in them a childhood which these old folk have not yet had. That

197

does not happen without a certain lack of respect, assuredly, but not without respect either. You go on, untameable, but with care. Forced to it. You go on, but the past in words awaits there in front of you. It mocks us. And that does not mean that you advance backwards, like Benjamin's angel. At any rate, it is only for the last of men, the nihilist, that the disaster of the *domus* and the rise of the megalopolis to the stars can procure an (evil) delight. Not only for the ingenious one who rushes ahead of what is coming in order to control it, but for his cousin, the well-meaning philosopher, who makes a virtue out of redundancy. It is impossible to think or write without some facade of a house at least rising up, a phantom, to receive and to make a work of our peregrinations. Lost behind our thoughts, the *domus* is also a mirage in front, the impossible dwelling. Prodigal sons, we engender its patriarchal frugality.

Thus things past are remembered ahead. The beginning, the awakening, offers itself only at the end as its inscription, by the writing of the remembrance, in its working-out. Always to be reread, redone. And the dwelling of the work is built only from this passage from awakening to the inscription of the awakening. And this passage itself does not cease to pass. And there is no roof where, at the end, the awakening will be over, where we will be awake, and the inscription will have ceased to inscribe. There is no *domus* as the rhyme of time, that is so. But nostalgia for the lost *domus* is what awakens, and our domain nowadays is the inscription of this awakening. So only transit, transfer, translation and difference. It is not the house passing away, like a mobile home or the shepherd's hut, it is in passing that we dwell.

The only kind of thought – but an abject, objective, rejective thought – which is capable of thinking the end of the *domus*, is perhaps the thought suggested by techno-science. The domestic monad was still almost 'naked', to use Leibniz's terms, not a large enough means of memorizing, practising, inscribing. It is decomposed as the big monad forms in its greater complexity, the one that Heidegger, coming from a quite other kind of thinking, from thinking which determined itself quite otherwise, names the *Gestell*. Much more complete, much more capable of programming, of neutralizing

198

the event and storing it, of mediating what happens, of conserving what has happened. Including, of course, and first of all, the untameable, the uncontrolled domestic remainder. End of tragedy, flexibility, permissiveness. The control is no longer territorialized or historicized. It is computerized. There is a process of complexification, they say, which is initiated and desired by no-one, no self, not even that of humanity. A cosmic zone, once called the earth, now a miniscule planet of a small stellar system in a galaxy of pretty moderate size – but a zone where neg-entropy is rife. The *domus* was too simple, it left too much remainder that it did not succeed in taming. The big techno-scientific monad has no need of our terrestial bodies, of passions and writings that used to be kept in the *domus*. What it needs is 'our' wonderful brains. When it evacuates the dying solar system, the big monad, which is cosmically competitive, will not take the untameable along with it. Before imploding, like the other celestial bodies, with its sun, little Earth will have bequeathed to the great spatial megalopolitan monad the memory that was momentarily confided to the most intelligent of earthly species. But the only one of any use for the navigation of the monad in the cosmos. So they say.

Metaphysics is realized in the physics, broad sense, operating in the techno-science of today. It certainly requires of us another mourning than the kind required by the philosophy of disaster and redundancy. The line taken is not that of the untameable, but of its neglect. To do the (quasi-Leibnizian) physics of the unconscious, we might say. No need for writing, childhood, pain. To think consists in contributing to the amelioration of the big monad. It is that which is obsessively demanded of us. You must think in a communicable way. Make culture. Not think according to the welcome of what comes about, singularly. To pre-vent it, rather. To success is to process.* Improve performances. It's a domestication, if you will, but with no *domus*. A physics with no god-nature. An economy in which everything is taken, nothing received. And so necessarily, an illiteracy. The respect and lack of respect of severe and serene reading of the

*In English in original. (Translators' note)

text, of writing with regard to language, this vast and still unexplored house, the indispensable comings and goings in the maze of its inhabited, always deserted rooms – the big monad doesn't give a damn about all this. It just goes and builds. Promotion. That's what it demands of humans. In the name of 'communicative action', 'conversation' and the relegation of philosophy, in the name of performativity, we are begged to think useful. Useful for the composition of the megalopolis. I'm amazed that this consensualist demand can still nowadays be picked up as though it emanated from the idea of the Enlightenment. Whereas it results from the complexification of material ensembles, say the ingenious.

There was still some *domus* in the metropolis, *polis-métèr*, city mother, *mater* and patrimony. The metropolis refers only to a size which exceeds the domestic scale. Filiation and concern for the past are not its forte. It is not a city but an *urbs*. An *urbs* become its own *orbs*. We were hoping for a *cosmopolitès*, there is no need for a *megapolitès*. We need ingenious people. As many monads as the enormous megalopolitan memory will allow must be combined. Its electrical circuits contain a power of which humans have no need and no idea: stored energy, and potential capacity. With the ancient idea of *dynamis*, the world was schematized like a nature, and nature like a *domus*. Domestic events in a unique, sensitive finality. As for the megalopolis, it conceives scenarios of cosmic exile by assembling particles.

Baudelaire, Benjamin, Adorno. How to inhabit the megalopolis? By bearing witness to the impossible work, by citing the lost *domus*. Only the quality of suffering counts as bearing witness. Including, of course, the suffering due to language. We inhabit the megalopolis only to the extent that we declare it uninhabitable. Otherwise, we are just lodged there. In the closure of time paid off (security), await the catastrophe of the instant, wrote Benjamin. In the inevitable transformation of works into cultural commodities, keep up a searing witness to the impossibility of the work, wrote Adorno. To inhabit the uninhabitable is the condition of the ghetto. The ghetto is the impossibility of the *domus*. Thought is not *in* the ghetto. Every work to which prodigal thought resolves itself *secretes* the wall of its ghetto, serves to neutralize thought. It can only

200

leave its trace upon the brick. Making media graffiti, ultimate prodigality, last homage to the lost frugality.

What domesticity regulated – savagery – it demanded. It had to have its off-stage within itself. The stories it tells speak only of that, of the *seditio* smouldering up at its heart. Solitude is *seditio*. Love is *seditio*. All love is criminal. It has no concern for the regulation of services, places, moments. And the solitude of the adolescent in the *domus* is seditious because in the suspense of its melancholy it bears the whole order of nature and culture. In the secrecy of his bedroom, he inscribes upon nothing, on the intimate surface of his diary, the idea of another house, of the vanity of any house. Like Orwell's Winston, he inscribes the drama of his incapacity before the law. Like Kafka. And lovers do not even have anything to tell. They are committed to *deixis*: this, now, yesterday, you. Committed to presence, deprived of representation. But the *domus* made legends and representations out of these silences and these inscriptions. In place of which the megalopolis displays, commentates on them, and explains them, makes them communicable. It calls melancholy being autistic and love sex. Like the way that it calls *fruges* agro-alimentry products. Secrets must be put into circuits, writings programmed, tragedies transcribed into bits of information. Protocols of transparency, scenarios of operationality. After all, I'll take it, your *domus*, it's saleable, your nostalgia, your love, let me get on with it. It might come in useful. The secret is capitalized swiftly and efficiently. – But that the secret should be a secret of nothing, be uncultivated, senseless, already in the *domus*, the megalopolis has no idea. Or rather, it has only the idea. Whereas the secret, because it consists only in the timbre of a sensitive, sentimental matter, is inaccessible except to stupor.

I wanted to say only this, it seems. Not that the *domus* is the figure of community that can provide an alternative to the megalopolis. Domesticity is over, and probably it never existed, except as a dream of the old child awakening and destroying it on awakening. Of the child whose awakening displaces it to the future horizon of his thoughts and writing, to a coming which will always have to be deferred. It is thus, not even like some surface of inscription which is there, well and truly there, but like an unknown astral body exercising its attraction on writing and thought from afar; rather, then, like a mirage which sets requirements than like a required condition – it is thus that the domestic world does not cease to operate on our passibility to writing, right up to the disaster of the houses. Thought today makes no appeal, cannot appeal, to the memory which is tradition, to bucolic *physis* to rhyming time, to perfect beauty. In going back to these phantoms, it is sure to get it wrong – what I mean is, it will make a fortune out of the retro distributed by the megalopolis just as well (it might come in useful). Thought cannot want its house. But the house haunts it.

The house does not haunt contemporary thought in the way that it once pierced the untameable, forcing it into the tragic mode. The untameable was tragic because it was lodged in the heart of the *domus*. The domestic schema resisted the violence of a timbre that was none the less irresistible. The tragic *cursus* stages this incommensurability, between the beautiful ordinance of a rhymed space-time and the amazement procured by the sublime encounter with an unprepared material, the tone of a voice, the nuance of an iris or a petal, the fragrance of a smell. A no-saying amid the always already said: stupor. A stupid passion rises in the domestic dough. As though the god were dropping the share he took in the common bake. Were letting the matter of time and space be touched in the raw. All the same, this abandon, this bankruptcy can still be taken up by the *domus*, it represents them as tragedy. Untameable dominated, sublime held to the rules of the beautiful, outside-the-law redestined. – Here is the reason why the megalopolis does not permit writing, inscribing, 'living' not only pastoral poems, but even tragedies. Having dispersed the domestic schemas. So the untameable is not representable there. Timbre is consigned by the megalopolis to the ghetto. And it's not the 'good old' ghetto tolerated by the *domus*, itself a somewhat domestic and domesticated ghetto. It is the Warsaw ghetto, administratively committed to *Vernichtung*, the 'rear' of the megalopolitan front. It must be exterminated because it constitutes an empty opacity for the programme of total mobilization in view of transparency.

Where the untameable finds a way of gripping on, is domestic flesh. Either it devastates it, or else the flesh reduces it, tames and eliminates it. They go together, in their insoluble *différend*. With Nazism the big monad in the process of forming mimicked the *domus*. Whence the exceptional tenacity, which arose from the (artificial) reconstitution of flesh. Does that remain a constant temptation, after Nazism? At any rate the untameable has to be controlled, if the big monad is to be competent and competitive. Everything must be possible, without remainder, with a bit of ingenuity. But that's just it, the *domus* isn't ingenious enough, the extermination betrays too much *hybris*, there has to be a more rational and open way of operating. More operational, less reactively earthly. Secrecy must not surround the destruction of the secret. Communication and culture accomplish this destruction, and much better. Timbre will get analyzed, its elements will be put into a memory, it will be reproduced at will, it may come in useful. The important thing is not that the result is a simulacrum: so was tragedy. The important thing is to dominate – not even that, to treat – everything that was rebellious to the *domus*, as much as possible. As to what's left, it is condemned to extinction, denied, *vernichtet*.

And I wanted to say this too. – Well, we say to ourselves (who, 'we'?), well, at least in the ghetto we shall go on. As far as it is possible. Thinking, writing, is, in our sense, to bear witness for the secret timbre. That this witnessing should make up an oeuvre and that this oeuvre might be able, in a few cases, at the price of the worst misunderstanding [*méprise*], of the worst contempt [*mépris*], to be placed on the circuits of the mediated megalopolis, is inevitable, but what is also inevitable is that the oeuvre promoted in this way be undone again, deconstructed, made redundant [*désoeuvrée*], deterritorialized, by the work of thinking some more, and by the bewildering encounter with a material (with the help not of god or of the devil, but of chance). Let us at least bear witness, and again, and for no-one, to thinking as disaster, nomadism, difference and redundancy. Let's write our graffiti since we can't engrave. – That seems to be a matter of real gravity. But still I say to myself: even the one who goes on bearing witness, and witness to what is condemned, it's that she isn't condemned, and that she survives the extermination of suffering. That she hasn't suffered enough, as when the suffering of having to inscribe what cannot be inscribed without a remainder is of itself the only grave witnessing. The witness of the wrongs and the suffering engendered by thinking's *différend* with what it does not manage to think, this witness, the writer, the megalopolis is quite happy to have him or her, his or her witnessing may come in useful. Attested, suffering and the untameable are as if already destroyed. I mean that in witnessing, one also exterminates. The witness is a traitor.

Index

Augustine, Saint 68, 90
avant-garde art 93, 98,
101, 103–7, 121,
124–8
avant-gardes 2, 78, 115,
135, 174, 176

babies, and mothers as
landscapes 189
Bataille, F. 55
Baudelaire, Charles
Pierre 105, 126,
200
Baudrilard 34
Baumgarten, Alexander
97–8, 176
Bayle, François 180
Be (Newman) 87,88
beautiful, aesthetics of
the 125, 138–9, 154
beauty
in art 138
feeling of 109
and photography 122,
123
and the sublime 95–6,
98, 99, 137
Beckett, Samuel 79
Beethoven, Ludwig
van 183
beginning, idea of in
Newman's
paintings 82
Being, in Heidegger 111,
113
being-now, in
music 176, 179
Benjamin, Walter 31,
63, 200
Bergson, Henri 36, 39,

40, 41–3, 44, 51,
146, 161
binary logic 15
Blanchot 147
Bloch, Ernst 32, 158
body
and Cartesian
mechanics 38
and mass 40
possibility of thought
without a 8–23
and soul 131
and time today 62
Boileau, Nicolas 84,
94–5, 96, 97
Borges 65
Bouhours, Père 95–6
Boulez, Pierre 170, 177,
180
brain, human, and time
today 61, 62
breaching 48–51, 52, 53,
54, 55, 57
Brenner, Hildegarde 104
Breton, André 105
Buren, Daniel 103, 146
Burke, Edmund 84–5,
88, 92, 93, 99–101

Cage, John 28, 169,
176, 177
capital
and the avant-garde
104–5, 106
and time today 66–7,
69–71, 71
Carnap, Rudolf 71, 73
Carnot, N. 22
Cartesian
mechanics 36–8